Easy Piano

EASY WAYS to PRAISE
2ND EDITION

ISBN 978-1-4950-7184-3

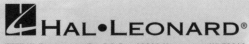

7777 W. Bluemound Rd. P.O. Box 13819 Milwaukee, WI 53213

Visit Hal Leonard Online at
www.halleonard.com

BROKEN VESSELS
(Amazing Grace)

Words and Music by JOEL HOUSTON
and JONAS MYRIN

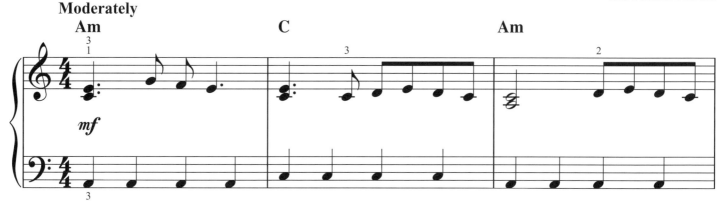

Oh, these piec - es, _____ bro - ken and
fail - ure, _____ You take our

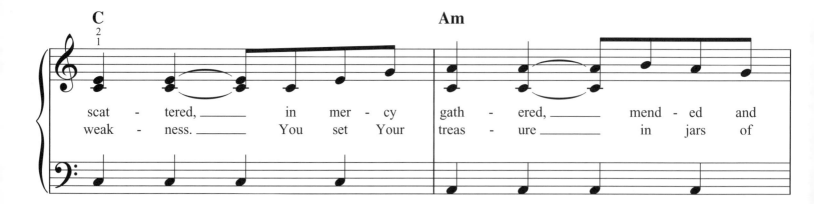

scat - tered, _____ in mer - cy
weak - ness. _____ You set Your

gath - ered, _____ mend - ed and
treas - ure _____ in jars of

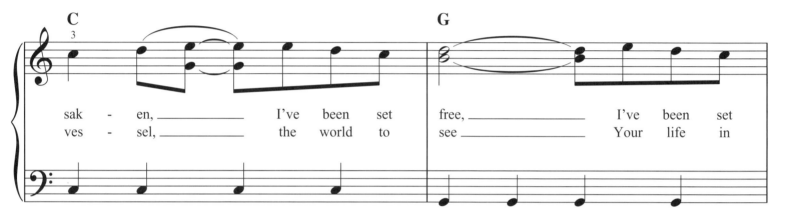

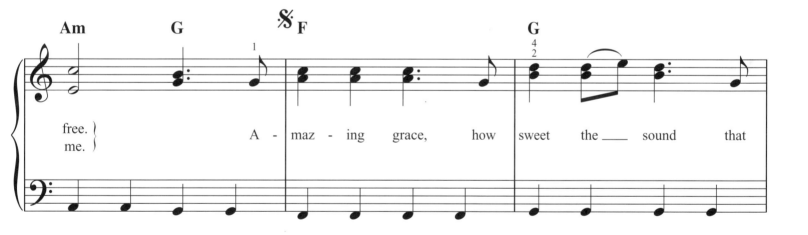

now I am found; was blind, but now I see. ___ Oh, I can see Your

love. ___ Oh, I can see the love ___ in ___ Your eyes, ___

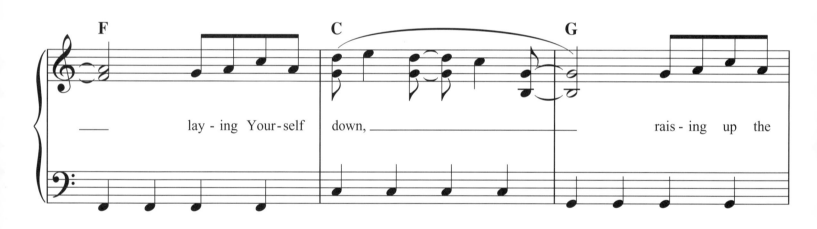

___ lay - ing Your-self down, ___ rais - ing up the

To Coda

bro - ken ___ to life. ___

You take our

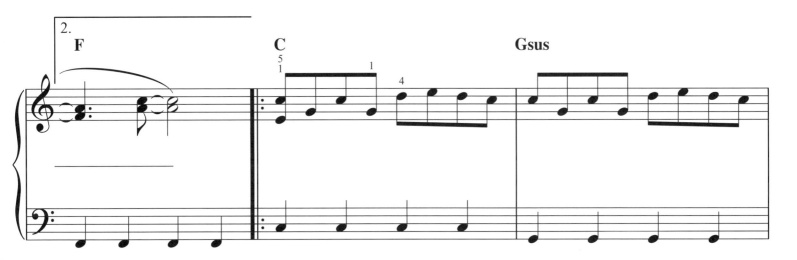

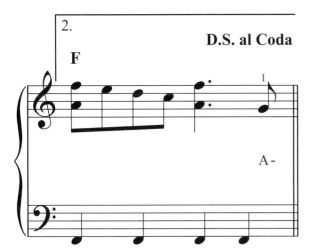

BUILD YOUR KINGDOM HERE

Words and Music by
REND COLLECTIVE

Upbeat Folk feel

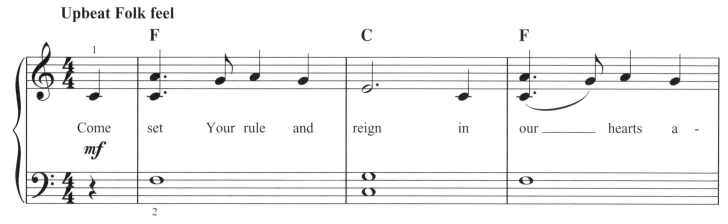

Come set Your rule and reign in our _____ hearts a-

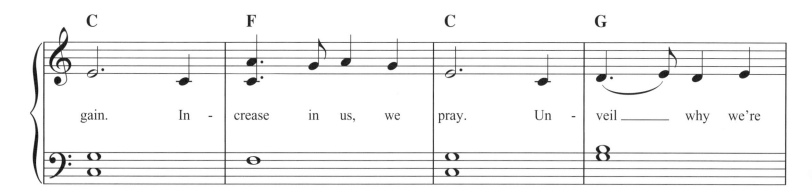

gain. In-crease in us, we pray. Un-veil _____ why we're

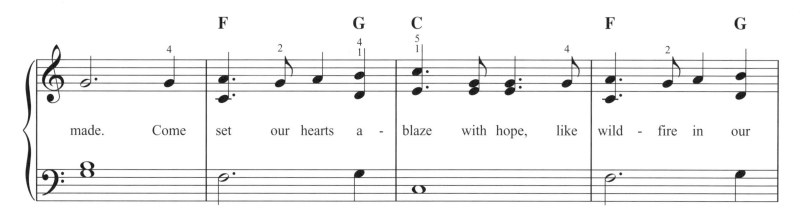

made. Come set our hearts a-blaze with hope, like wild-fire in our

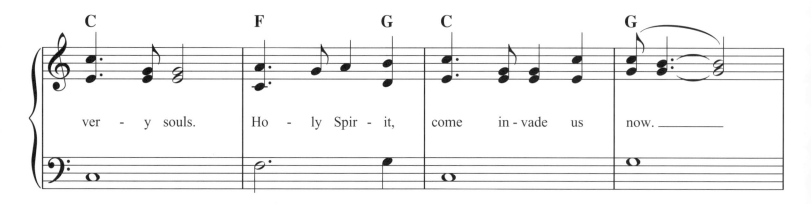

ver-y souls. Ho-ly Spir-it, come in-vade us now. _____

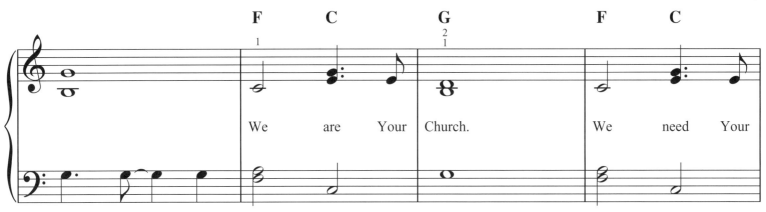

We are Your Church. We need Your

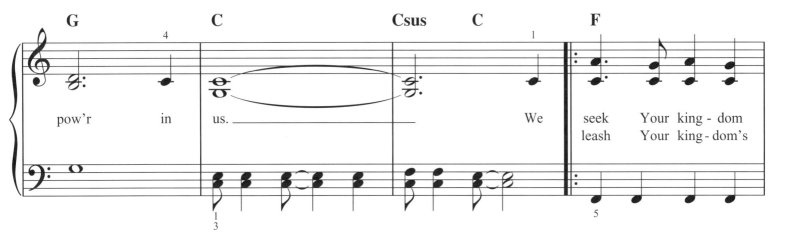

pow'r in us. _____ We seek Your king - dom
leash Your king - dom's

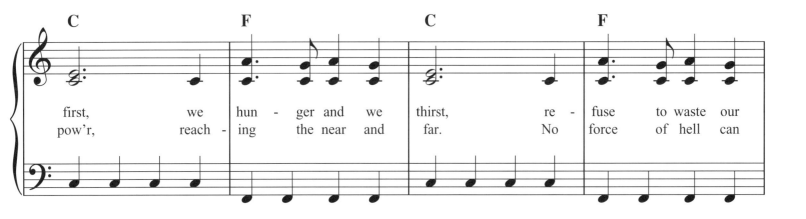

first, we hun - ger and we thirst, re - fuse to waste our
pow'r, we reach - ing the near and far. No force of hell can

lives, for You're our joy and prize. To see the cap - tive
stop Your beau - ty chang - ing hearts. You made us for much

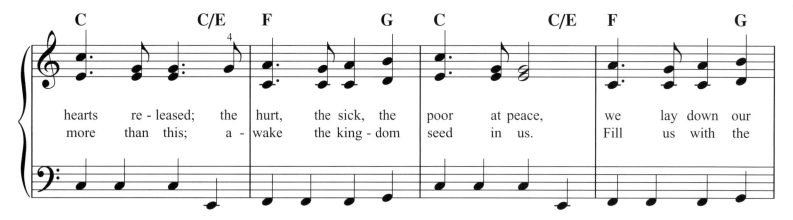

hearts re - leased; the hurt, the sick, the poor at peace, we lay down our
more than this; a - wake the king - dom seed in us. Fill us with the

lives for heav - en's cause. _____ We are Your
strength and love of Christ. _____ We are Your

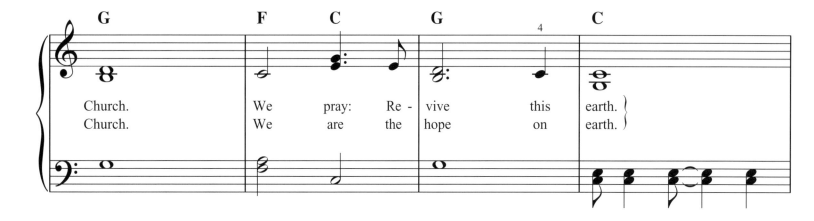

Church. We pray: Re - vive this earth.
Church. We are the hope on earth.

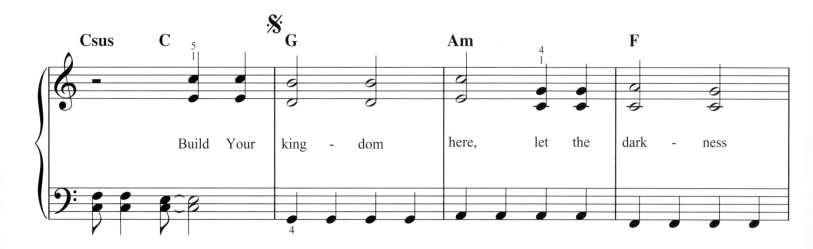

Build Your king - dom here, let the dark - ness

fear. Show Your might - y _____ hand, heal our streets and

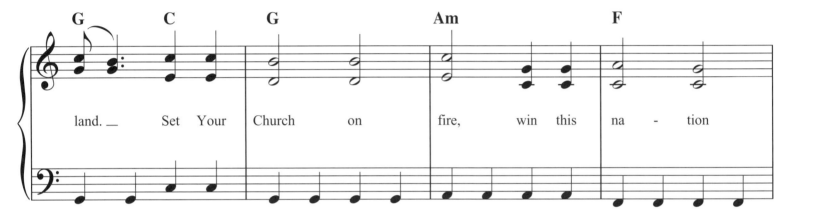

land. _ Set Your Church on fire, win this na - tion

To Coda ⊕

back. Change the at - mos - phere, build Your king - dom

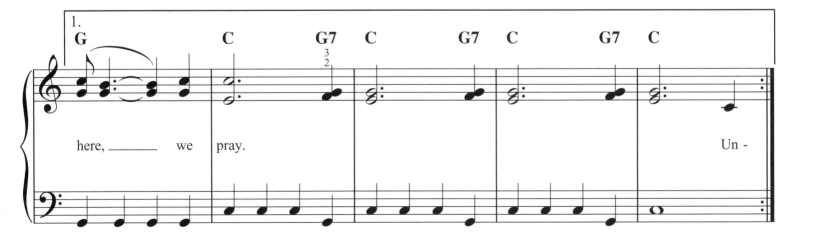

here, _____ we pray. Un -

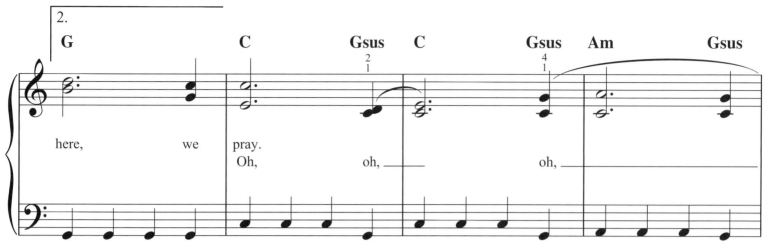

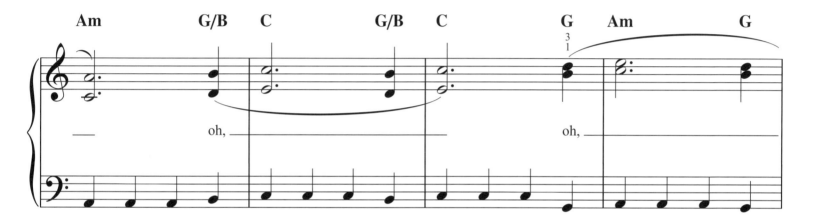

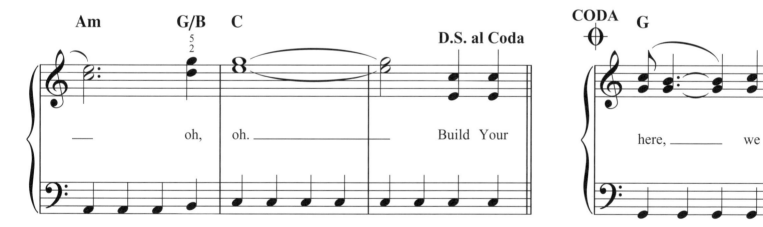

BECAUSE HE LIVES, AMEN

Words and Music by WILLIAM J. GAITHER,
GLORIA GAITHER, DANIEL CARSON,
CHRIS TOMLIN, ED CASH, MATT MAHER
and JASON INGRAM

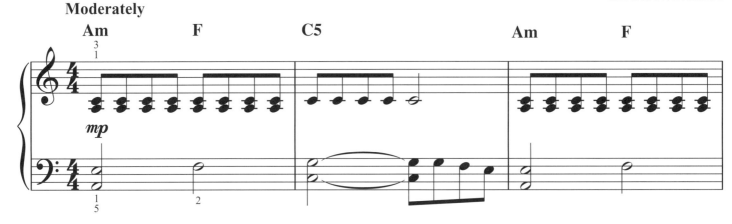

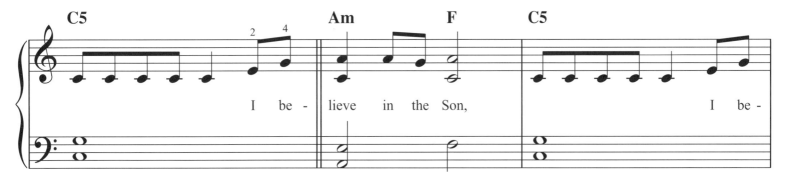

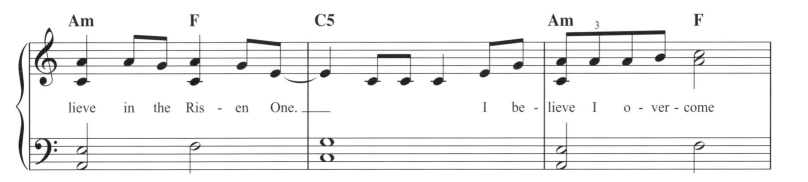

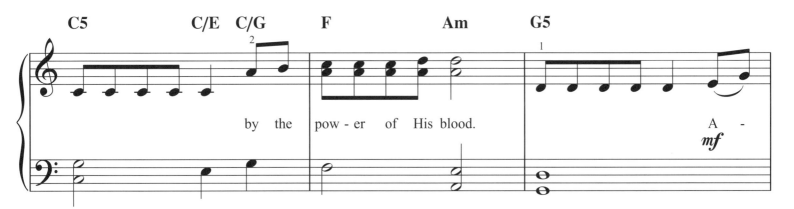

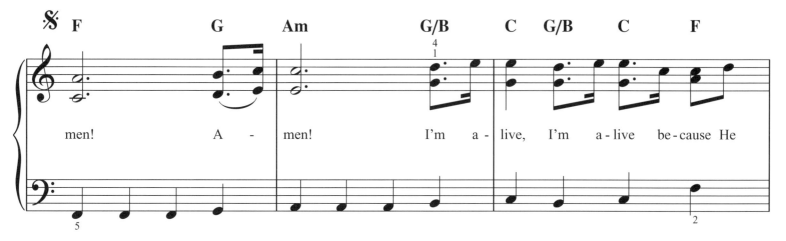

men! A - men! I'm a - live, I'm a - live be-cause He

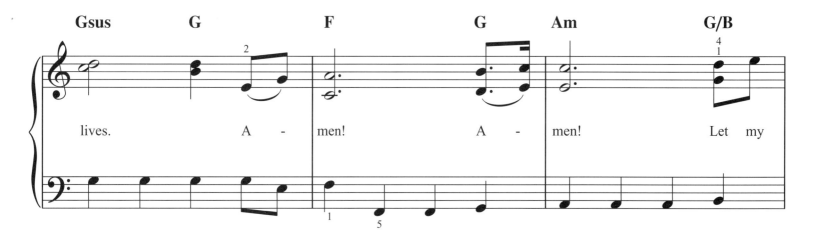

lives. A - men! A - men! Let my

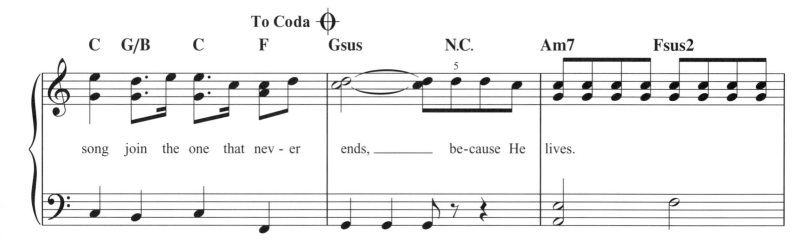

song join the one that nev - er ends, _____ be-cause He lives.

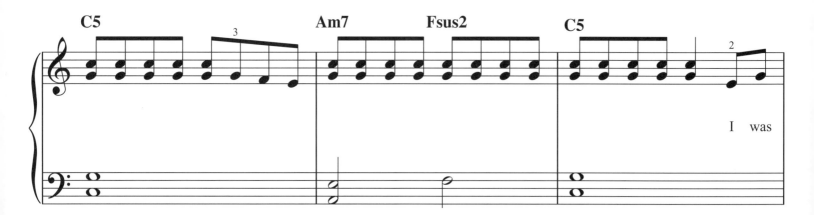

I was

dead in the grave, I was cov-ered in sin and shame. __

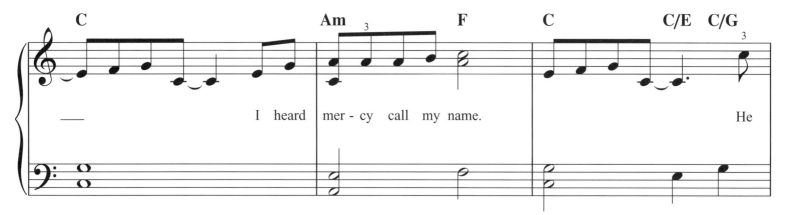

__ I heard mer-cy call my name. He

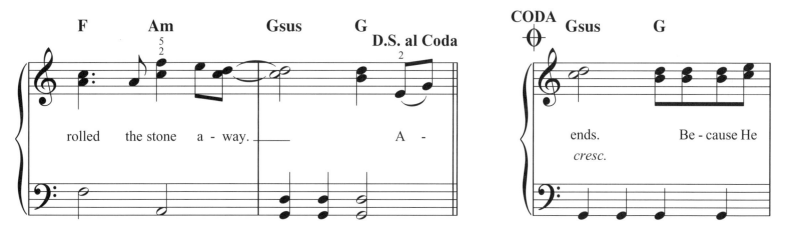

rolled the stone a - way. _____ A -

CODA

ends. Be - cause He
cresc.

lives, I can face to-mor-row. _____ Be-cause He lives, ev-'ry fear is

f

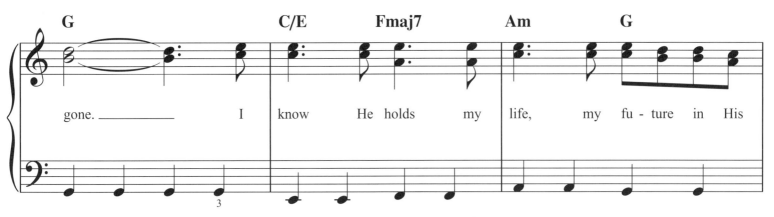

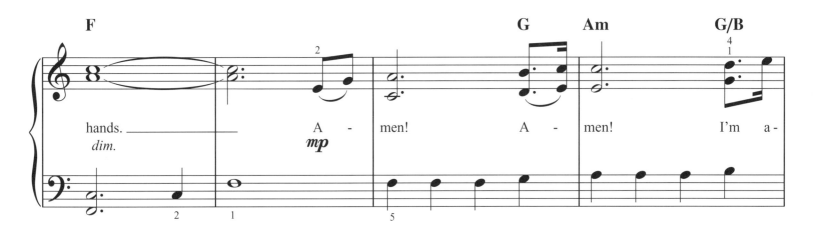

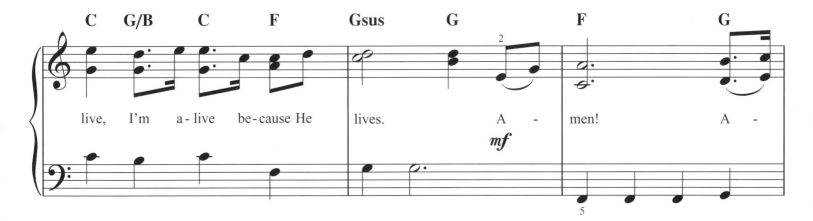

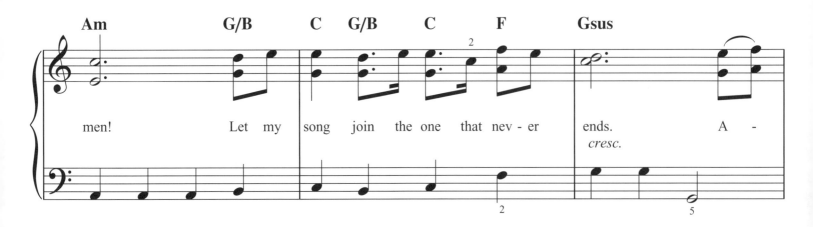

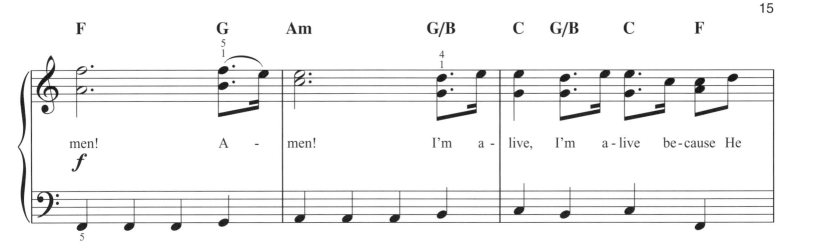

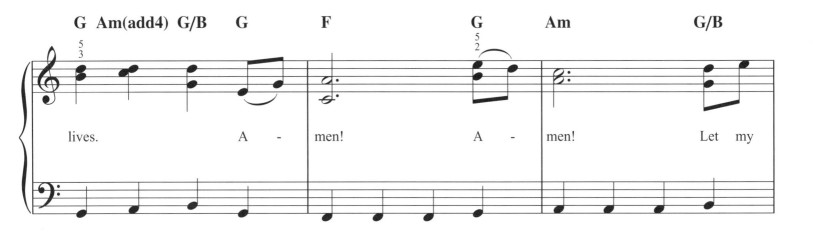

COME, NOW IS THE TIME TO WORSHIP

Words and Music by
BRIAN DOERKSEN

Driving Rock

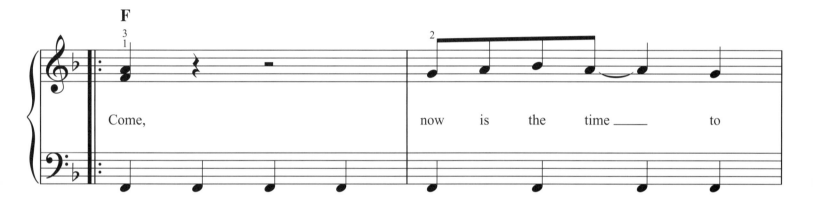

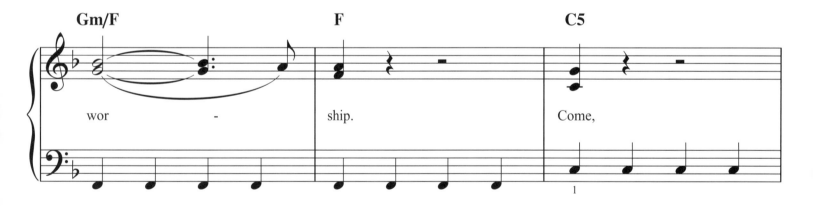

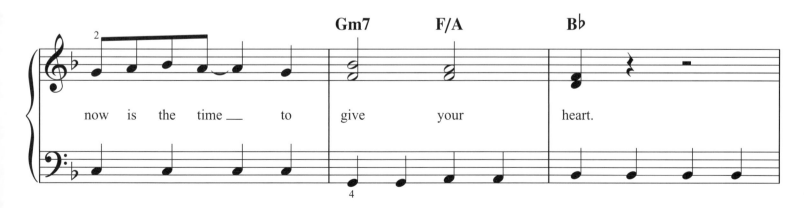

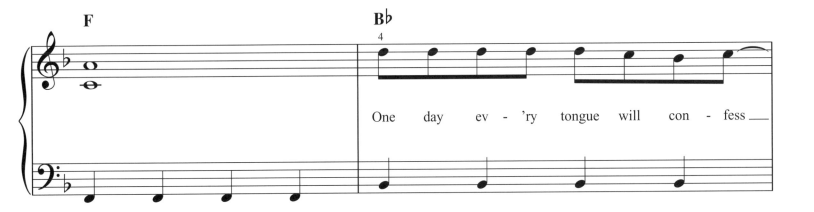

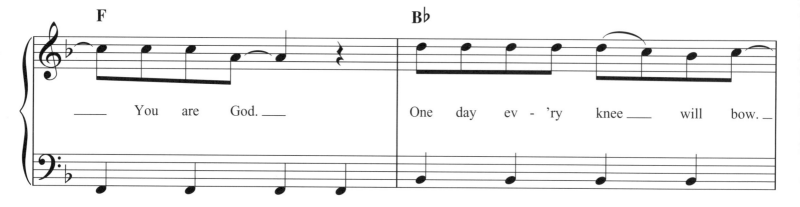

You are God. ____ One day ev - 'ry knee ____ will bow. __

____ Still the great - est treas - ure re - mains __

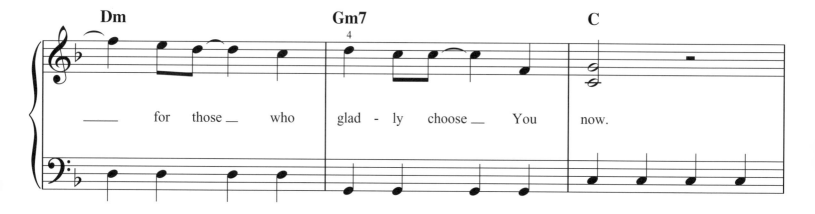

____ for those __ who glad - ly choose __ You now.

1.

2.

Come.

DAYS OF ELIJAH

Words and Music by
ROBIN MARK

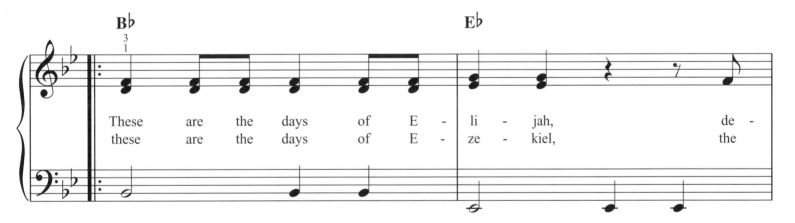

These are the days of E - li - jah, de -
these are the days of E - ze - kiel, the

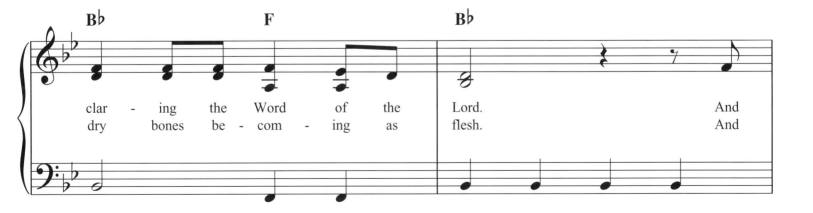

clar - ing the Word of the Lord. And
dry bones be - com - ing as flesh. And

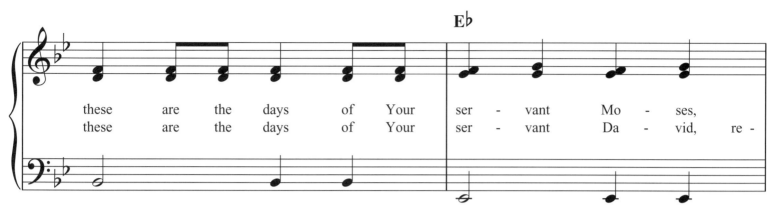

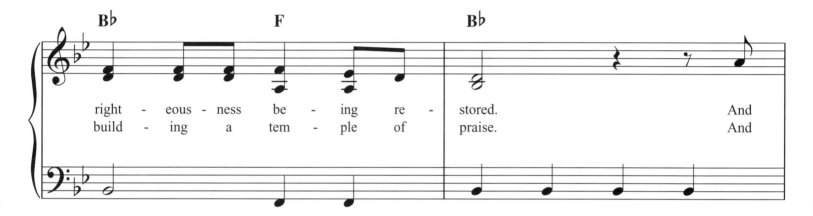

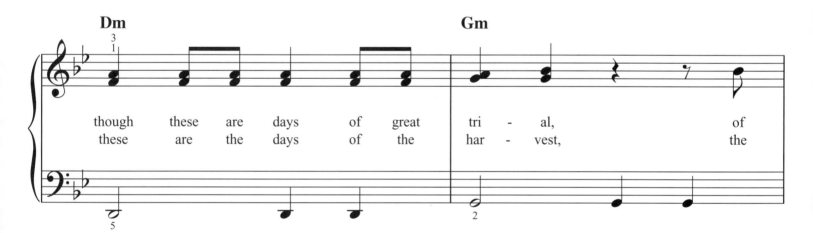

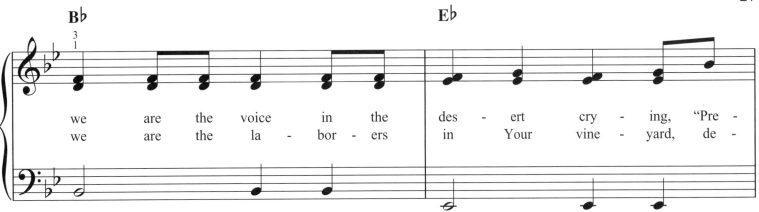

we are the voice in the des - ert cry - ing, "Pre -
we are the la - bor - ers in Your vine - yard, de -

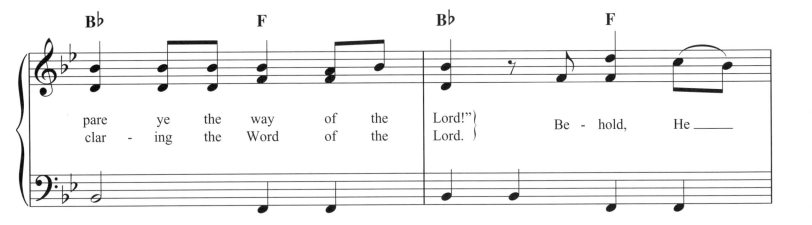

pare ye the way of the Lord!"
clar - ing the Word of the Lord. Be - hold, He _____

comes, rid - ing on the clouds, shin - ing like the

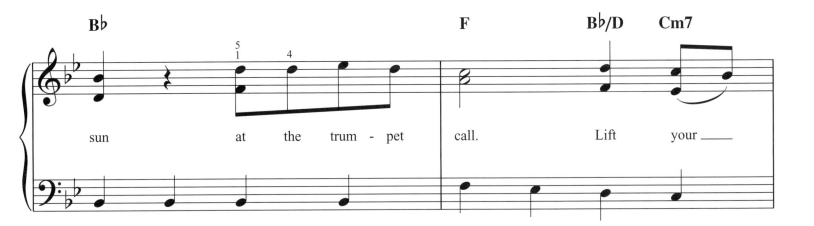

sun at the trum - pet call. Lift your _____

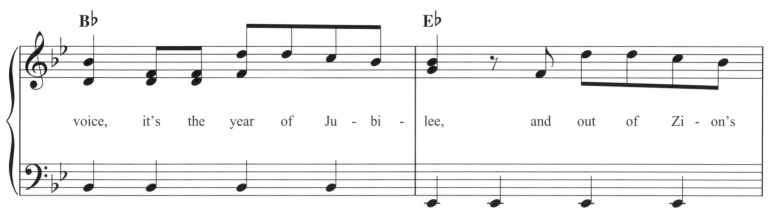

voice, it's the year of Ju - bi - lee, and out of Zi - on's

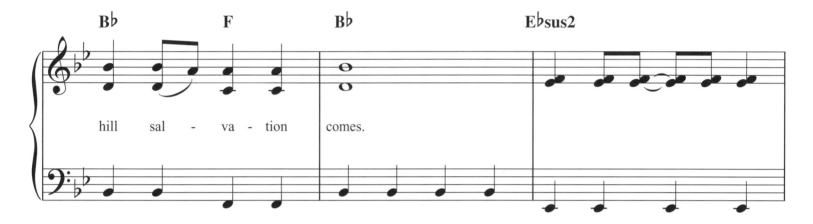

hill sal - va - tion comes.

1.

And

2.

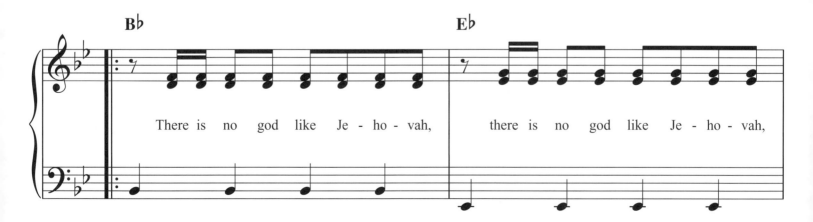

There is no god like Je - ho - vah, there is no god like Je - ho - vah,

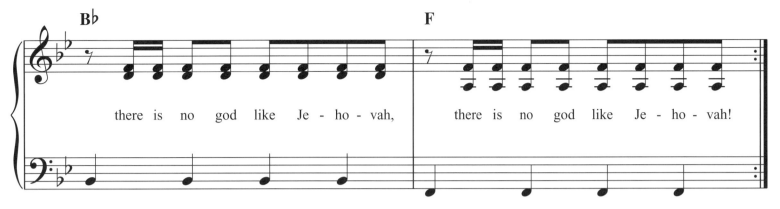

there is no god like Je - ho - vah, there is no god like Je - ho - vah!

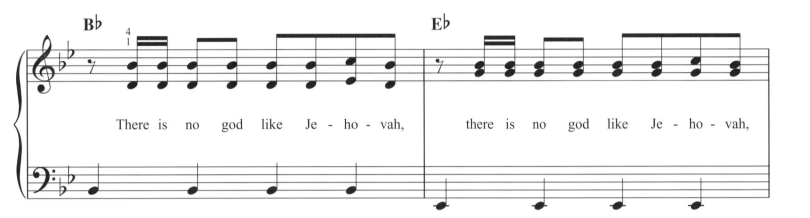

There is no god like Je - ho - vah, there is no god like Je - ho - vah,

there is no god like Je - ho - vah, there is no god like Je - ho - vah!

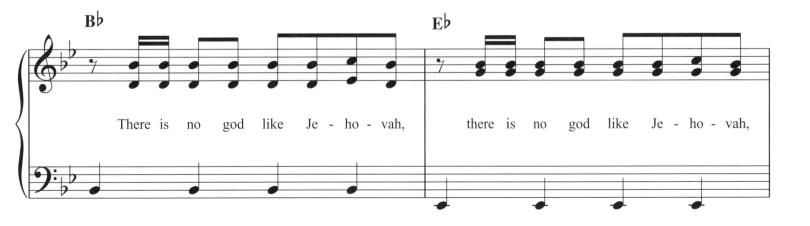

There is no god like Je - ho - vah, there is no god like Je - ho - vah,

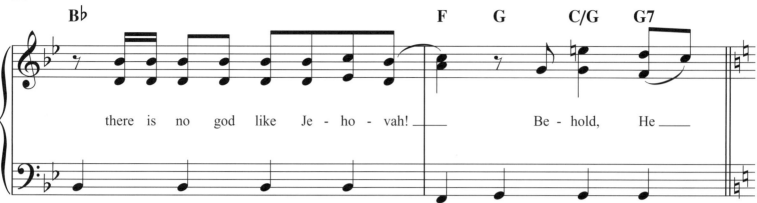

there is no god like Je - ho - vah! ____ Be - hold, He ____

comes, rid - ing on the clouds, shin - ing like the

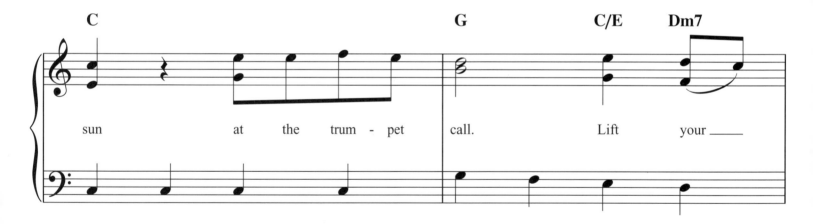

sun at the trum - pet call. Lift your ____

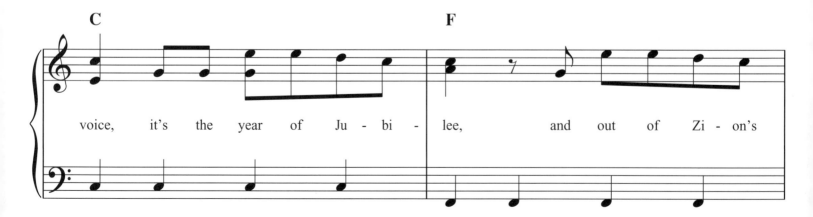

voice, it's the year of Ju - bi - lee, and out of Zi - on's

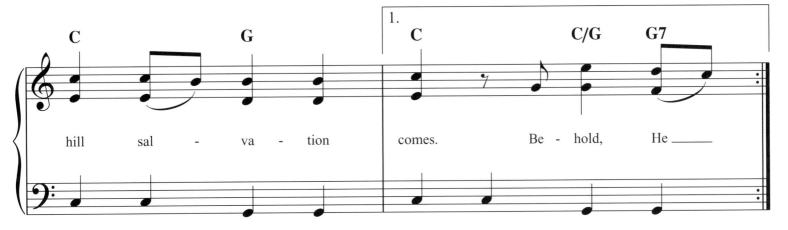

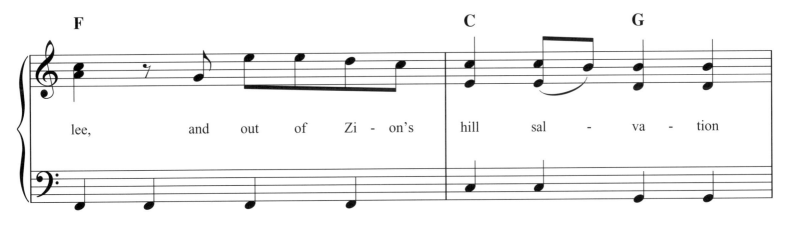

THE HEART OF WORSHIP
(When the Music Fades)

Words and Music by
MATT REDMAN

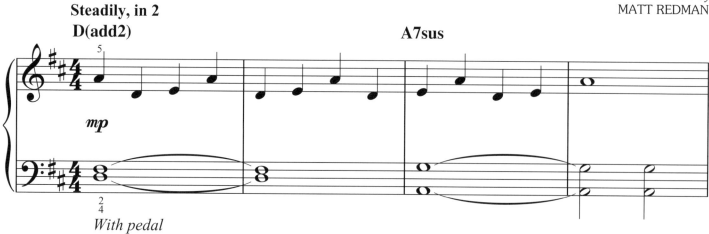

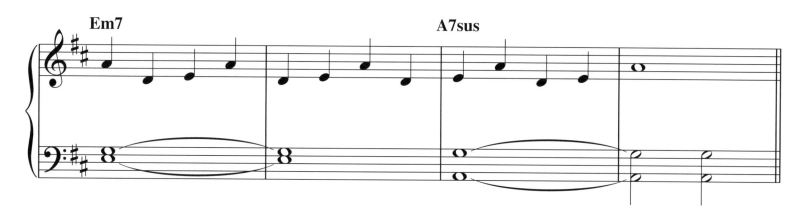

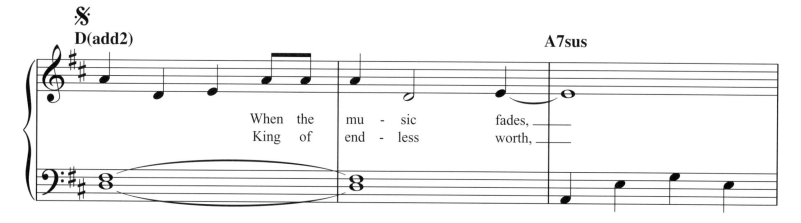

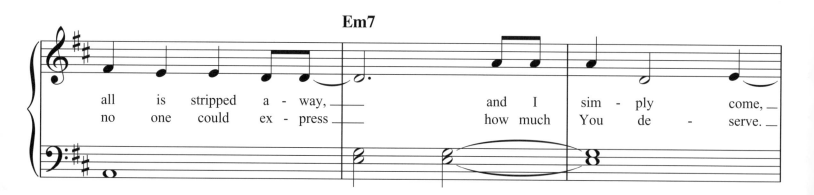

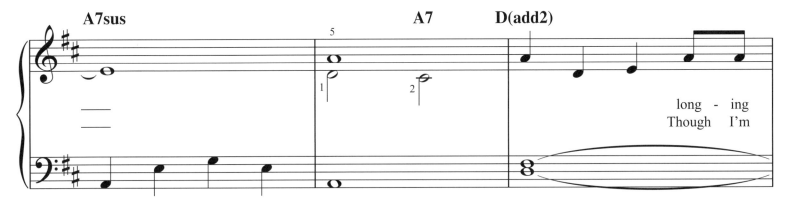

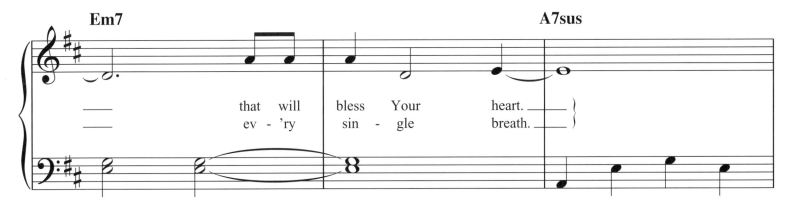

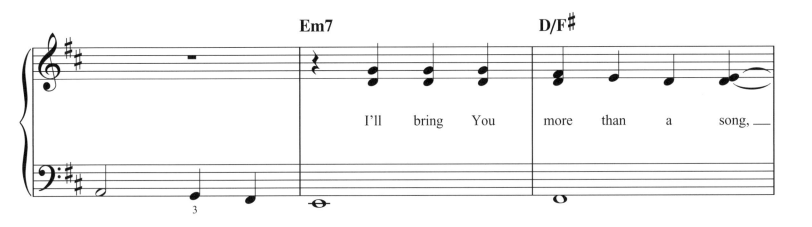

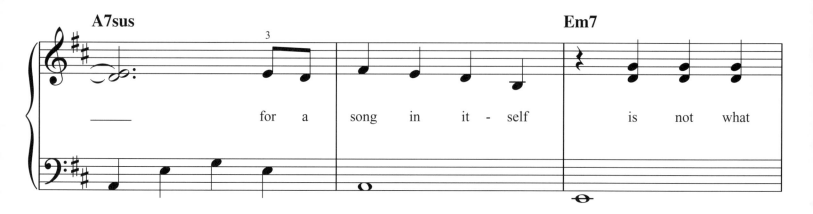

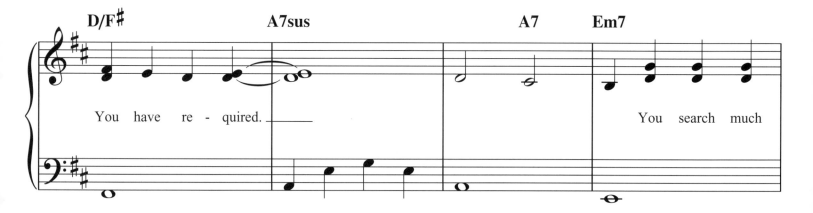

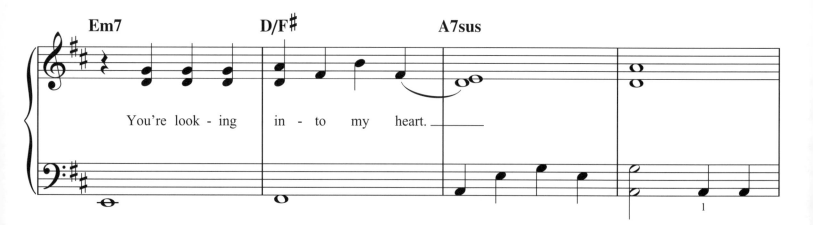

I'm com - ing back to the heart of wor -

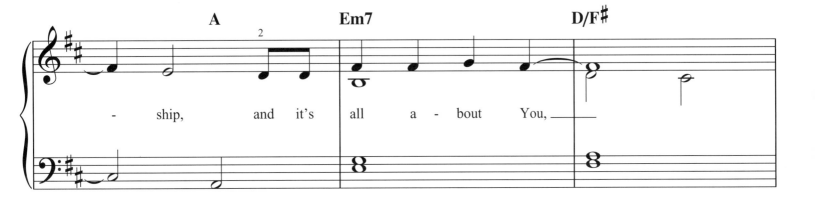

- ship, and it's all a - bout You, ____

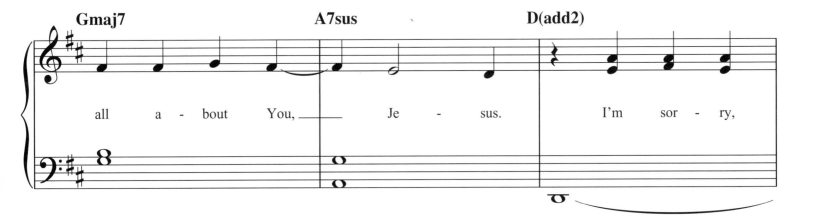

all a - bout You, ____ Je - sus. I'm sor - ry,

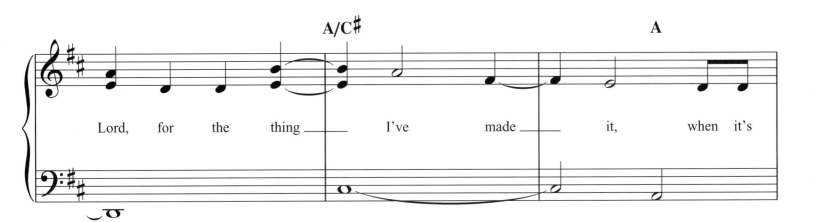

Lord, for the thing ____ I've made ____ it, when it's

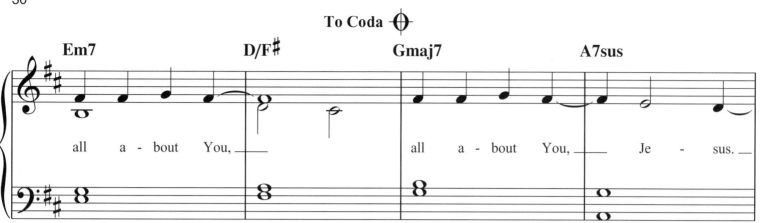

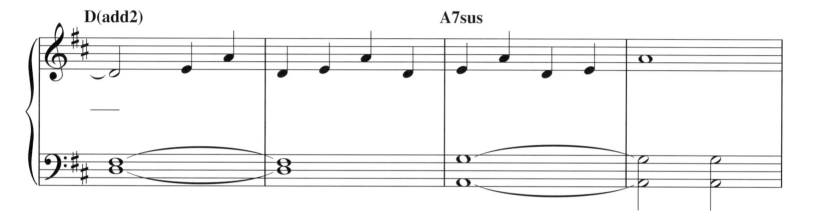

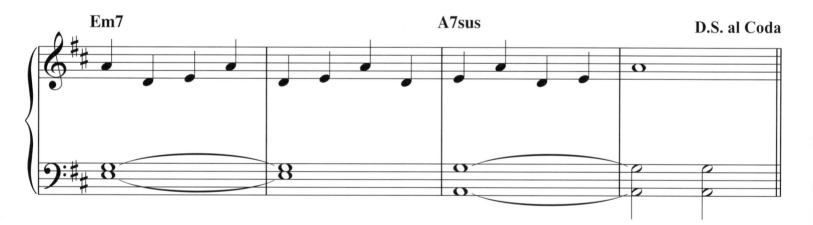

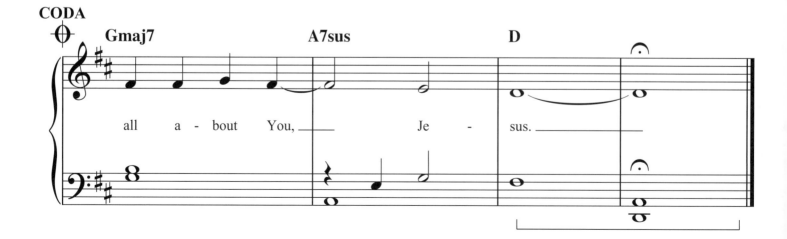

LORD, I LIFT YOUR NAME ON HIGH

Words and Music by
RICK FOUNDS

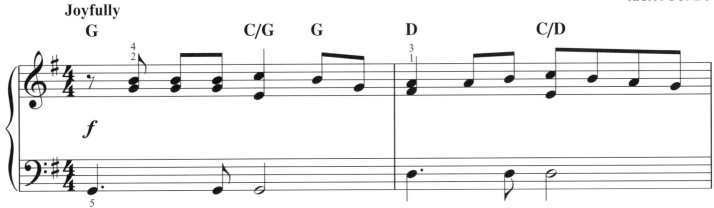

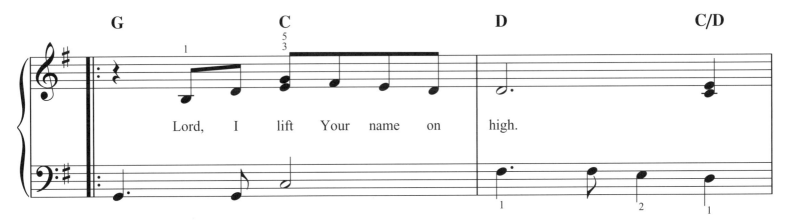

Lord, I lift Your name on high.

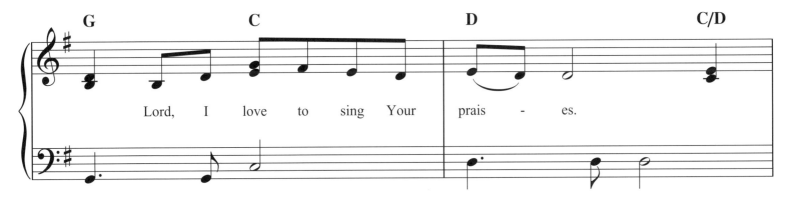

Lord, I love to sing Your prais - es.

I'm so glad You're in my life,

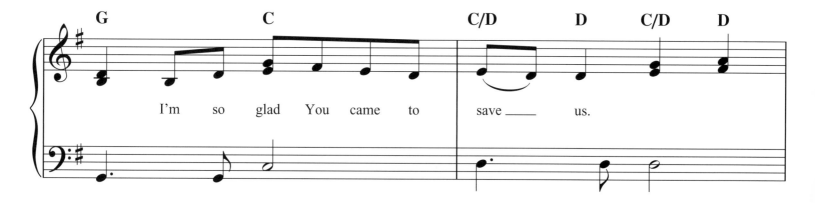

I'm so glad You came to save ___ us.

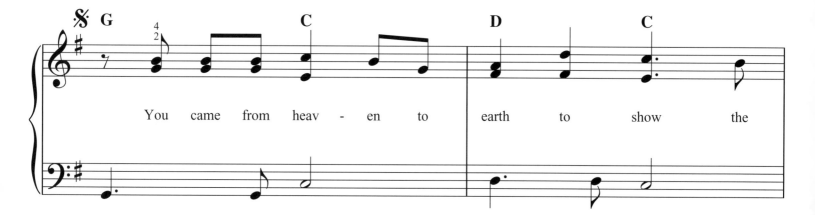

You came from heav - en to earth to show the

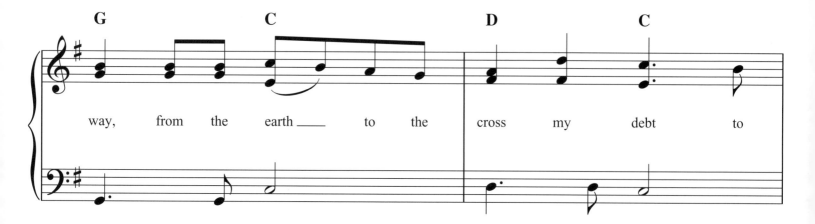

way, from the earth ___ to the cross my debt to

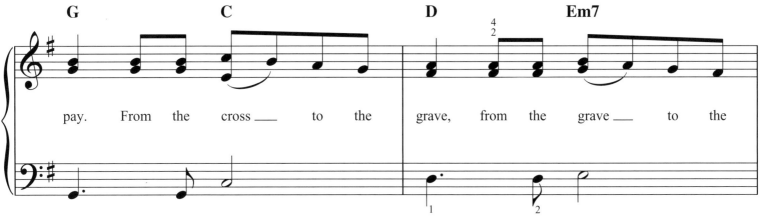

pay. From the cross ___ to the   grave, from the grave ___ to the

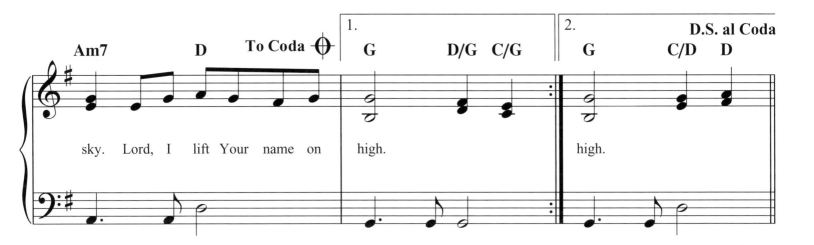

sky. Lord, I lift Your name on   high.   high.

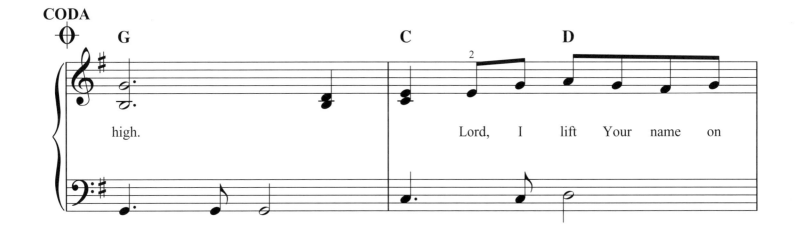

high.   Lord, I lift Your name on

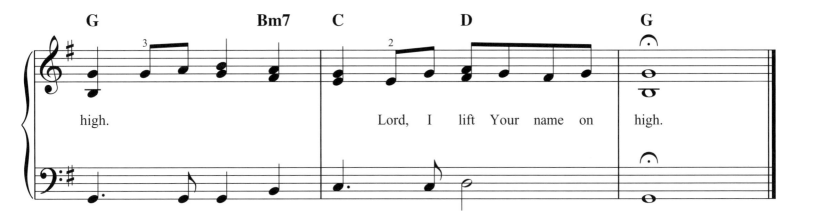

high.   Lord, I lift Your name on   high.

HOLY SPIRIT

Words and Music by KATIE TORWALT
and BRYAN TORWALT

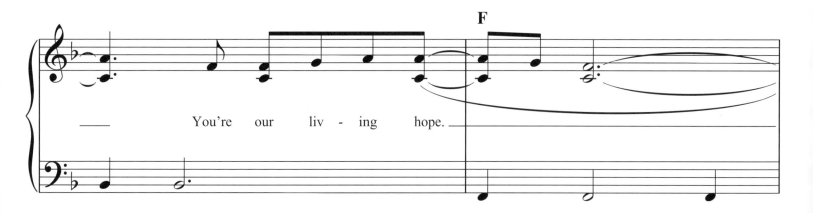

Your pres - ence, Lord.

I've tast - ed and seen ____ of the sweet - est of loves, __

____ where my heart be - comes free ____ and my shame is un - done. __

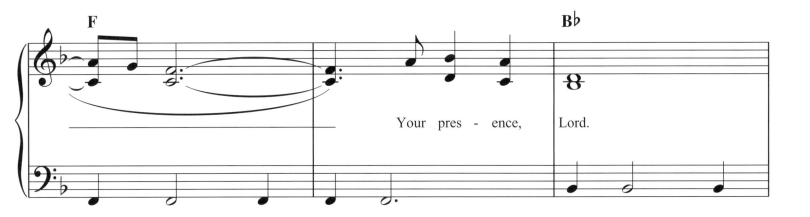

____ Your pres - ence, Lord.

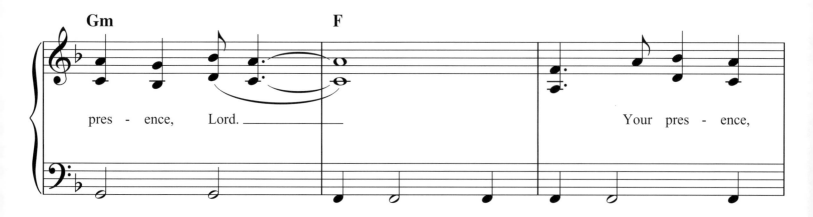

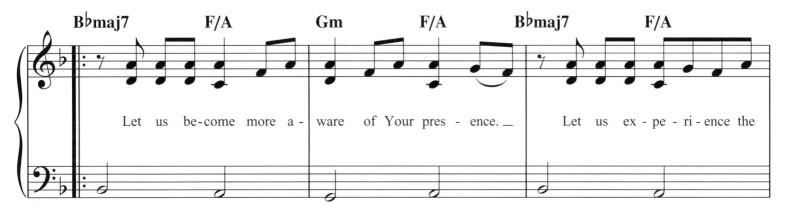

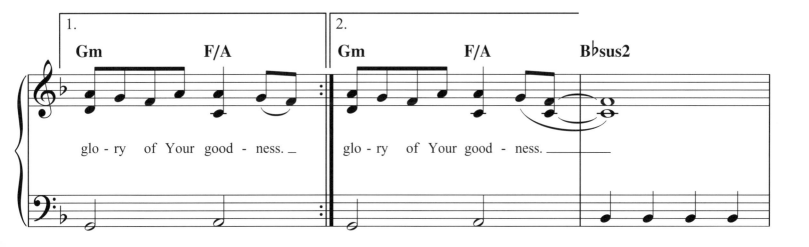

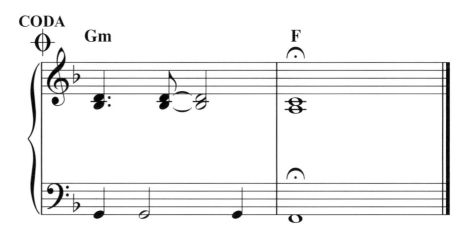

OPEN THE EYES OF MY HEART

Words and Music by
PAUL BALOCHE

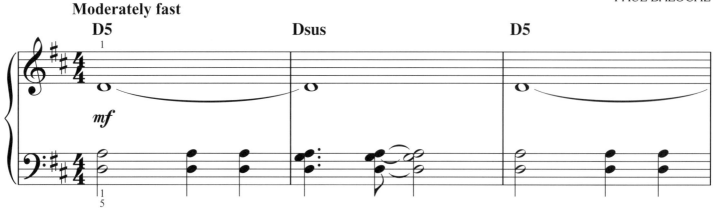

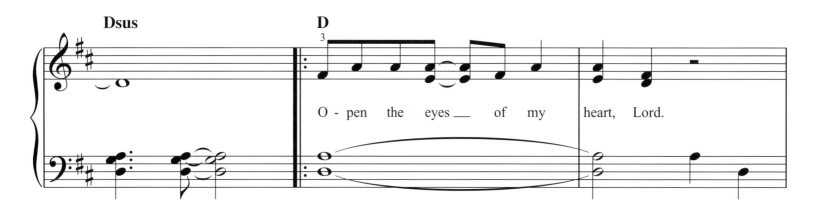

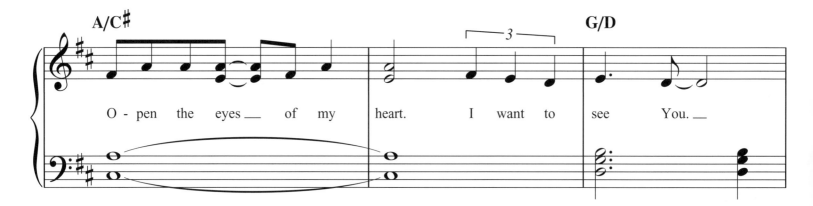

O - pen the eyes __ of my heart, Lord. O - pen the eyes __ of my

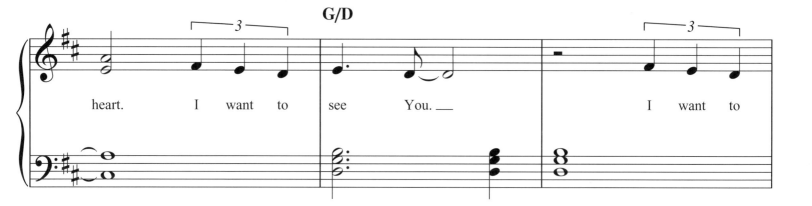

heart. I want to see You. __ I want to

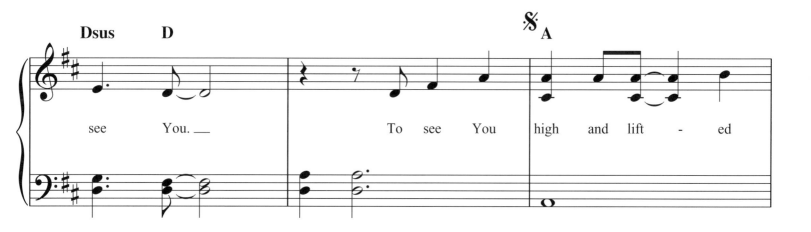

see You. __ To see You high and lift - ed

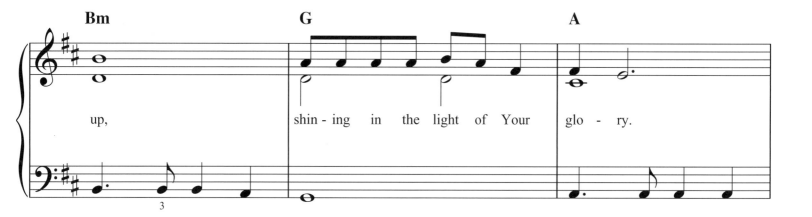

up, shin - ing in the light of Your glo - ry.

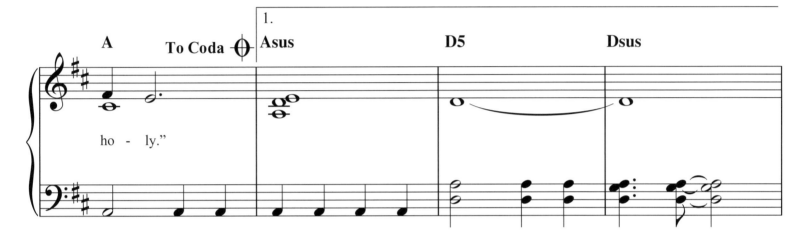

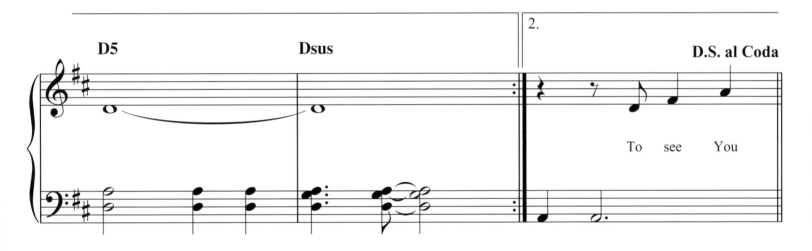

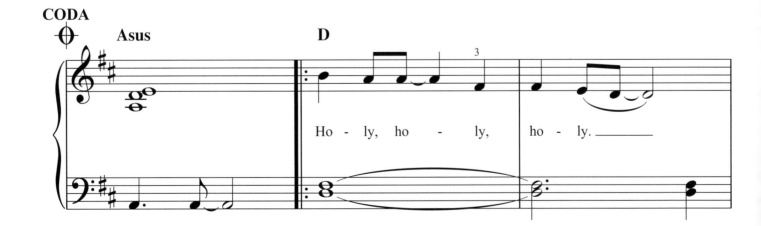

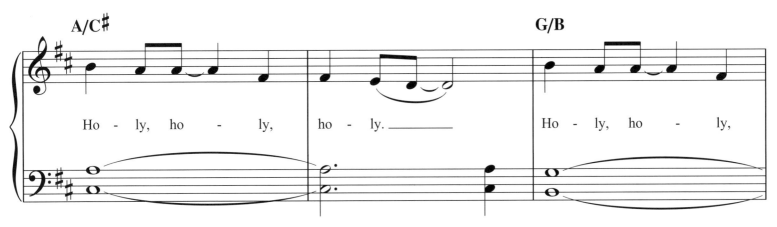

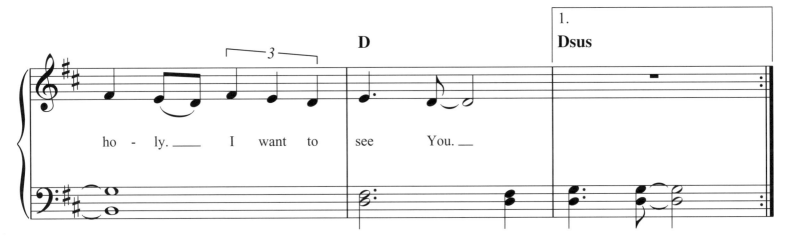

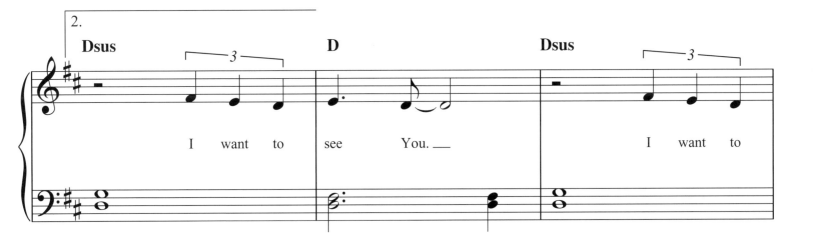

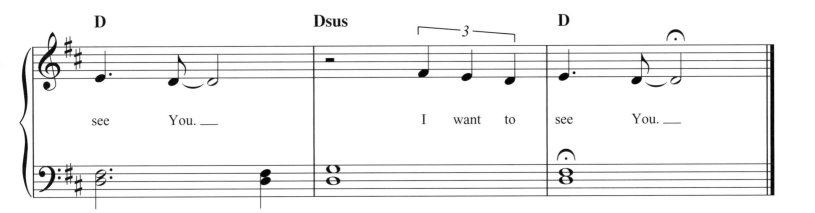

SHINE, JESUS, SHINE

Words and Music by
GRAHAM KENDRICK

With excitement

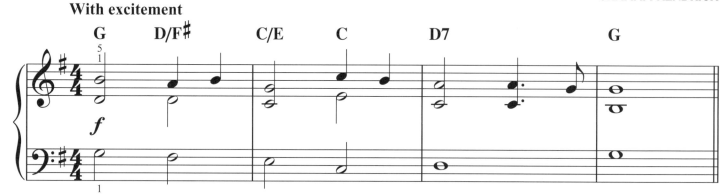

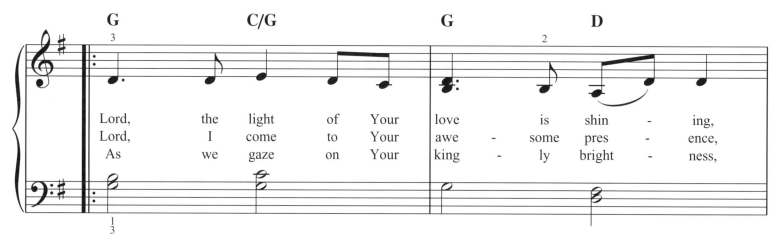

Lord, the light of Your love is shin - ing,
Lord, I come to Your awe - some pres - ence,
As we gaze on Your king - ly bright - ness,

in the midst of the dark - ness shin - ing.
from the shad - ows in - to Your ra - diance.
so our fac - es dis - play Your like - ness.

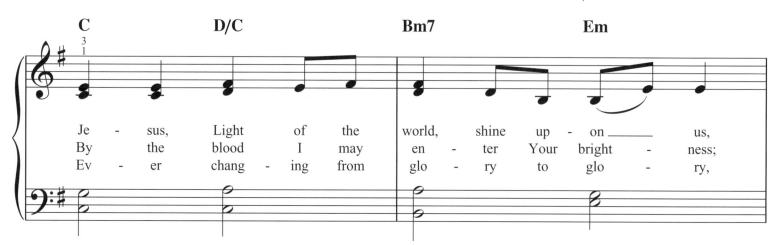

Je - sus, Light of the world, shine up - on us,
By the blood I may en - ter Your bright - ness;
Ev - er chang - ing may from glo - ry to glo - ry,

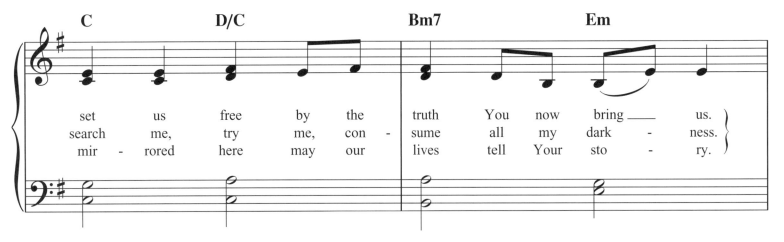

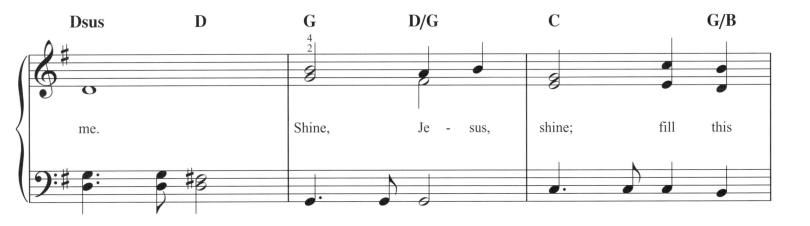

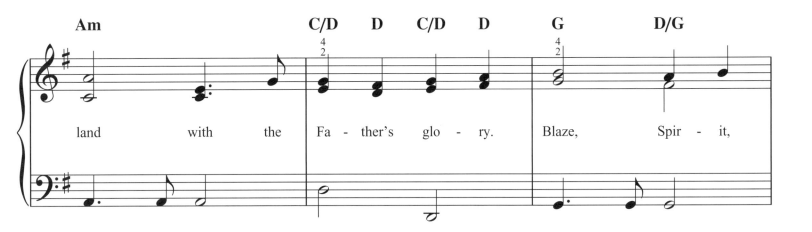

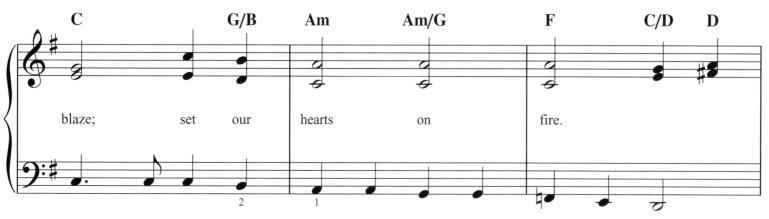

blaze;   set   our   hearts   on   fire.

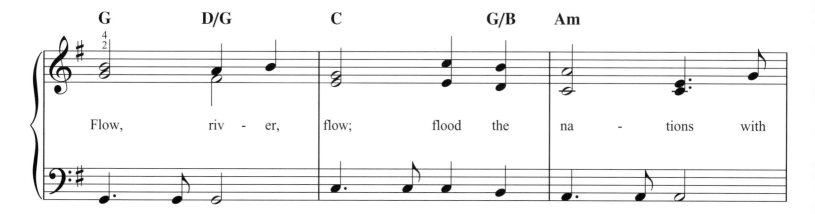

Flow,   riv - er,   flow;   flood   the   na - tions   with

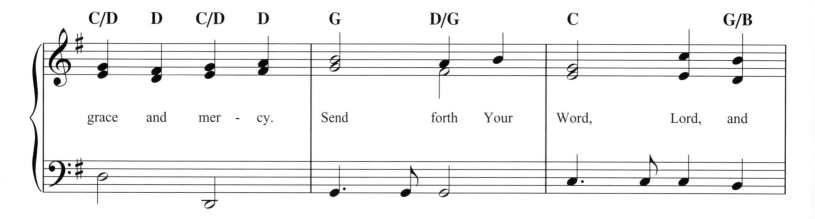

grace   and   mer - cy.   Send   forth   Your   Word,   Lord,   and

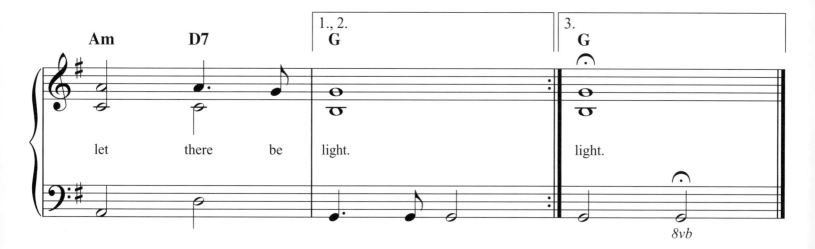

let   there   be   light.   light.

YOU'RE WORTHY OF MY PRAISE

Words and Music by
DAVID RUIS

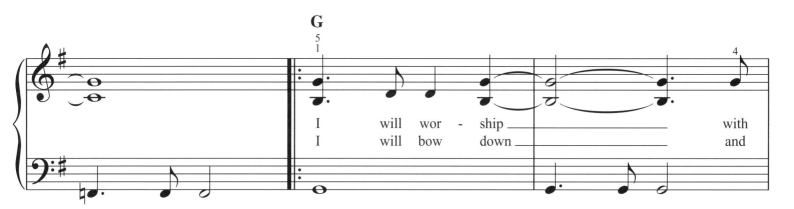

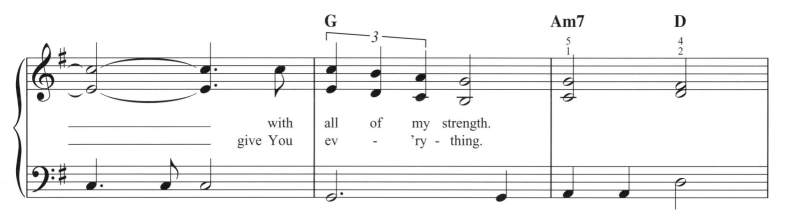

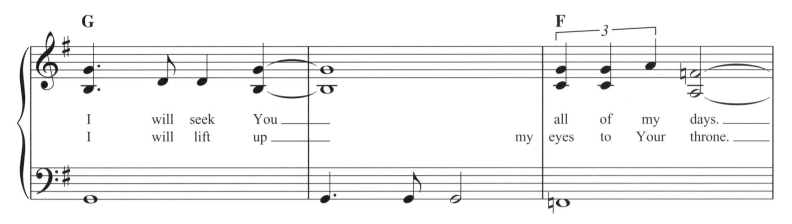

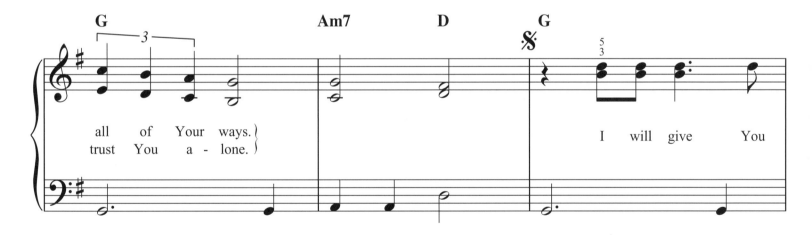

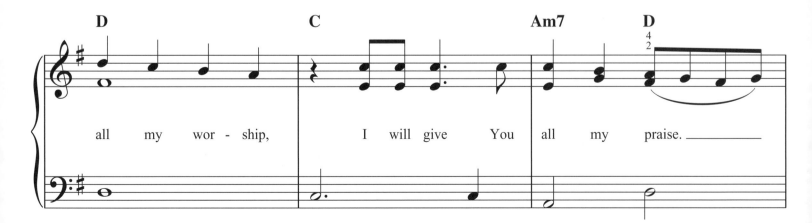

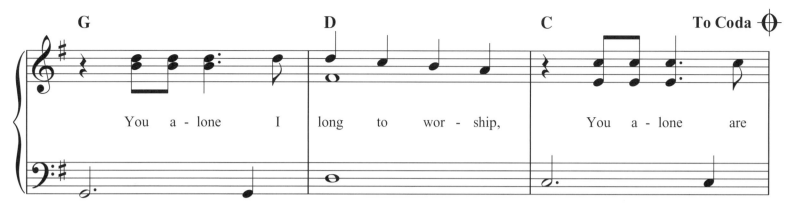

You a - lone I long to wor - ship, You a - lone are

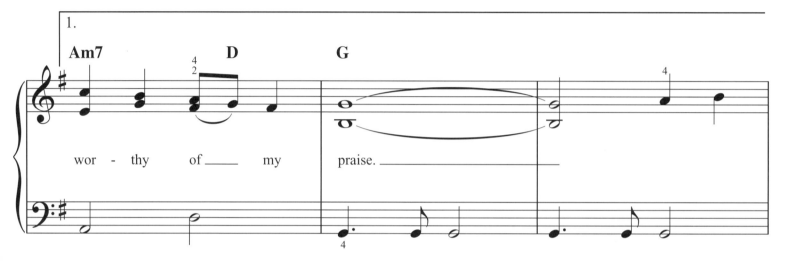

1.

wor - thy of ___ my praise. ___

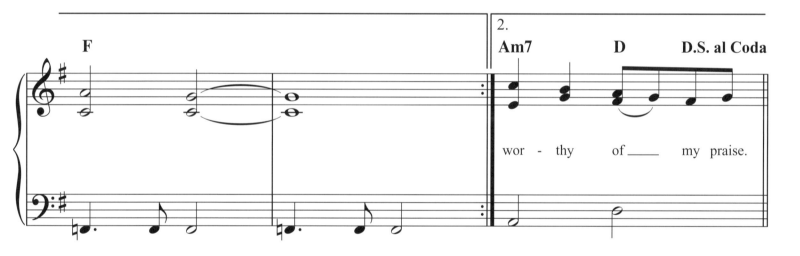

wor - thy of ___ my praise.

2.

D.S. al Coda

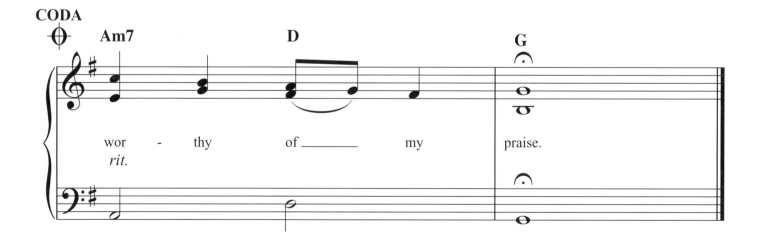

CODA

wor - thy of ___ my praise.

rit.

THIS I BELIEVE

(The Creed)

Words and Music by BEN FIELDING
and MATT CROCKER

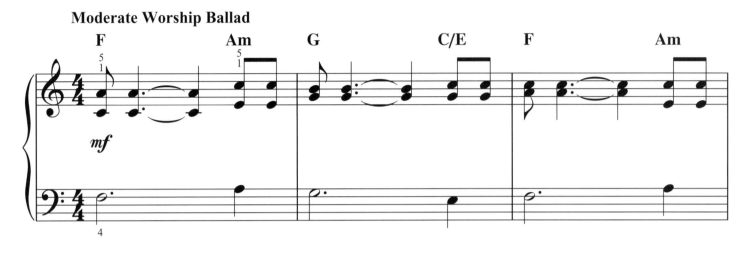

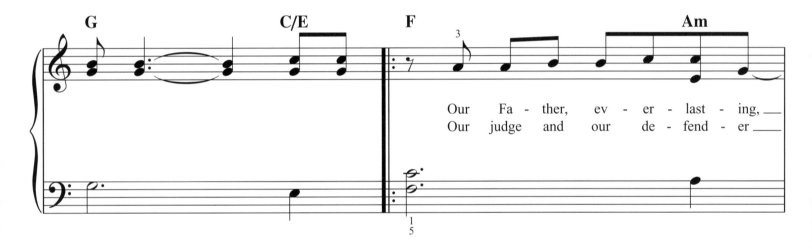

Our Father, ever-last-ing,___
Our judge and our de-fend-er ___

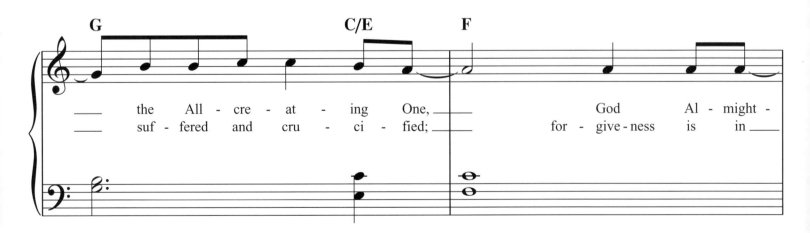

the All-cre-at-ing One,___
suf-fered and cru-ci-fied;

God Al-might-i
for-give-ness is in ___

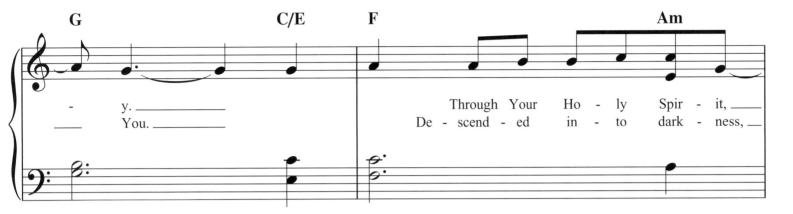

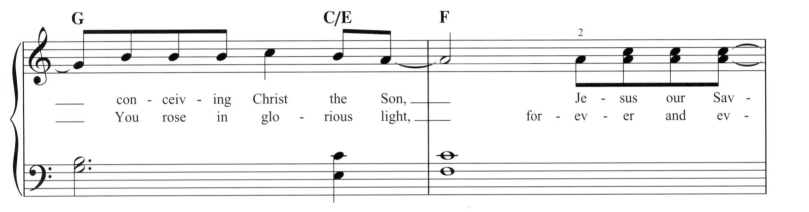

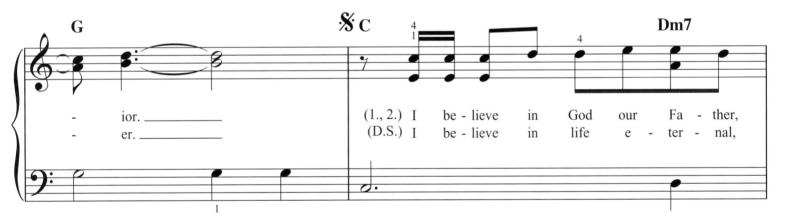

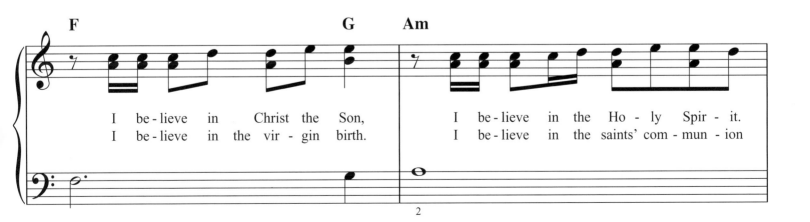

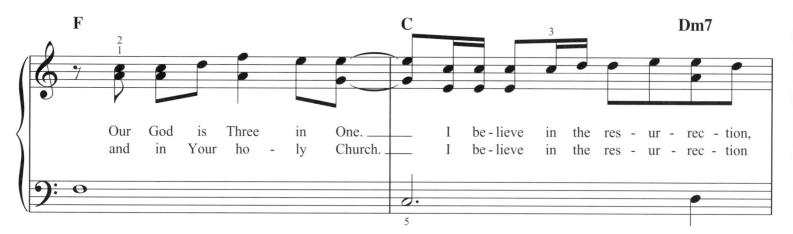

Our God is Three in One. _____ I be - lieve in the res - ur - rec - tion,
and in Your ho - ly Church. _____ I be - lieve in the res - ur - rec - tion

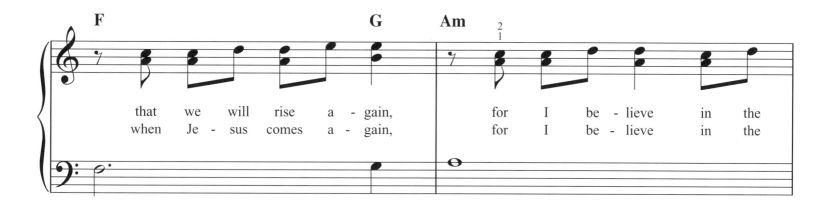

that we will rise a - gain, for I be - lieve in the
when Je - sus comes a - gain, for I be - lieve in the

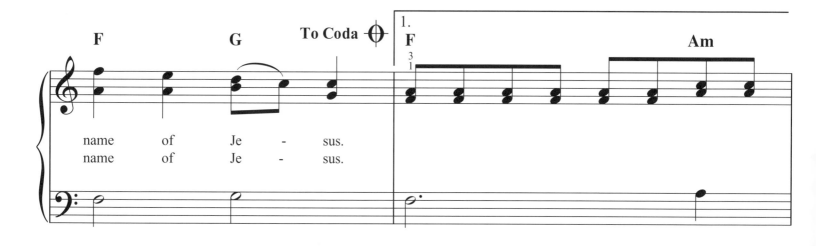

name of Je - sus.
name of Je - sus.

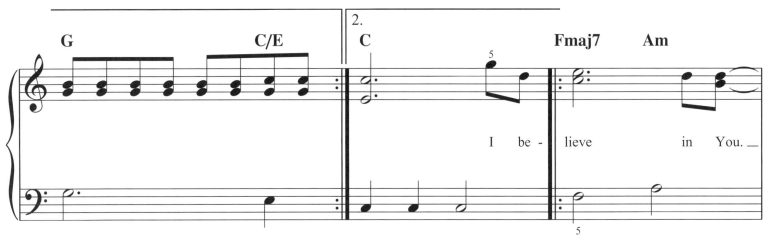

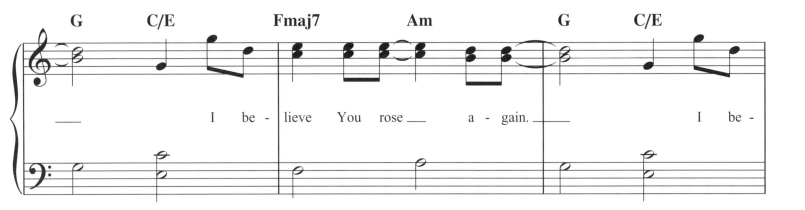

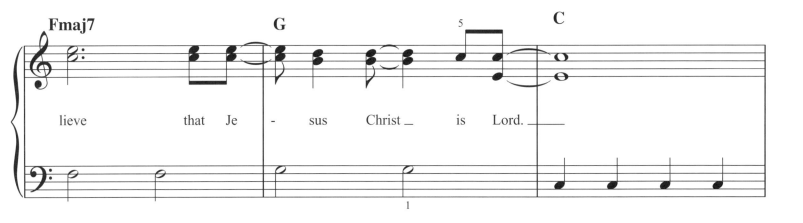

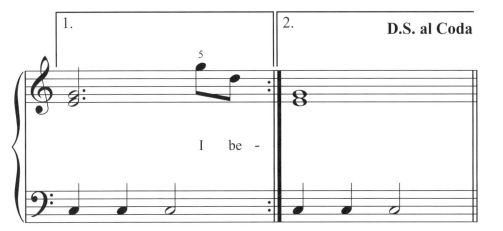

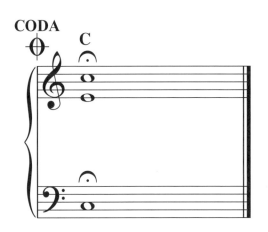

WE BELIEVE

Words and Music by TRAVIS RYAN,
MATTHEW HOOPER and RICHIE FIKE

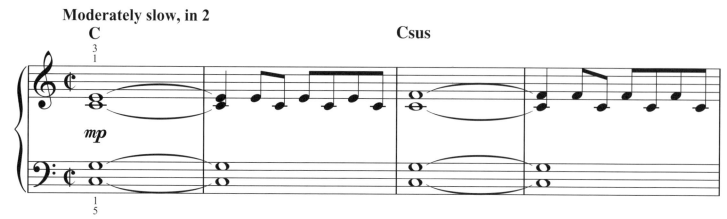

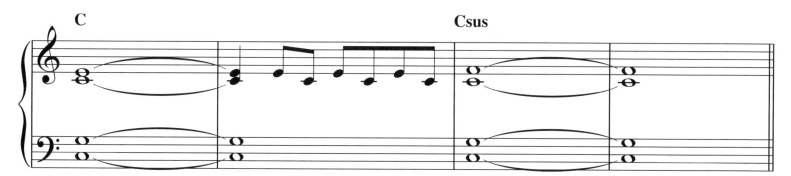

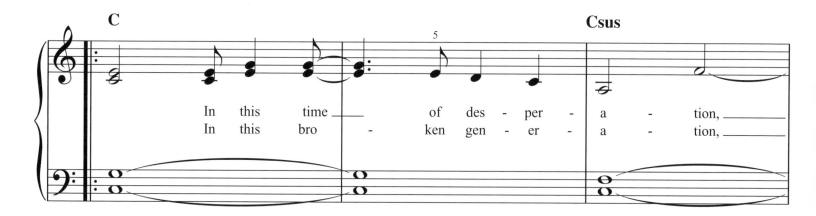

In this time ____ of des - per - a - tion, ____
In this bro - ken gen - er - a - tion, ____

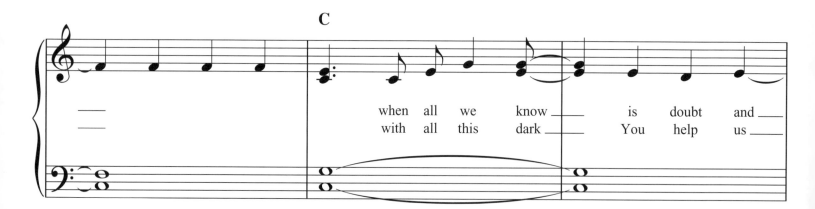

____ when all we know ____ is doubt and
____ with all this dark ____ You help us

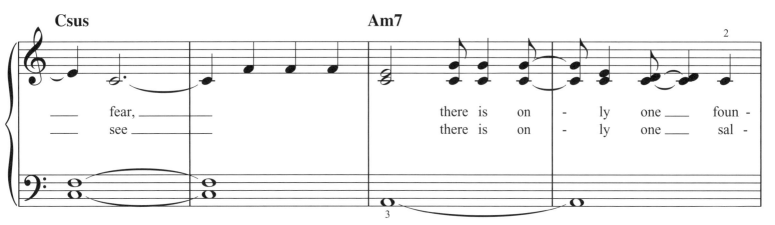

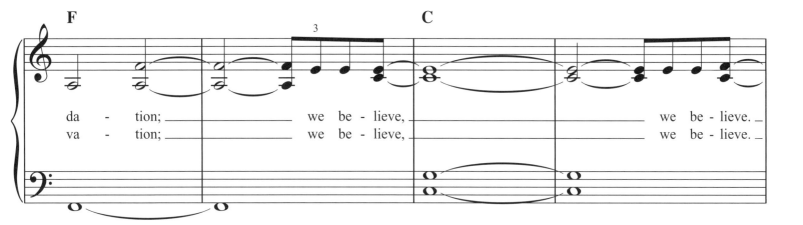

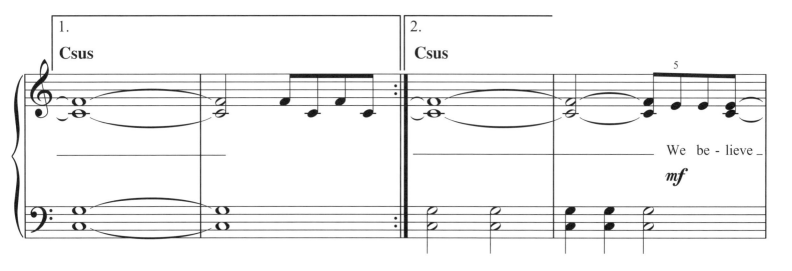

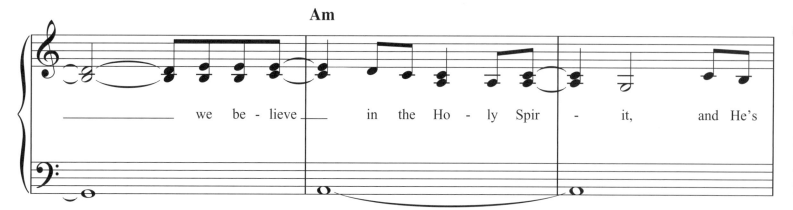

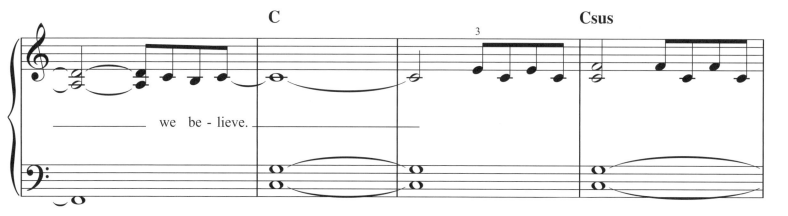

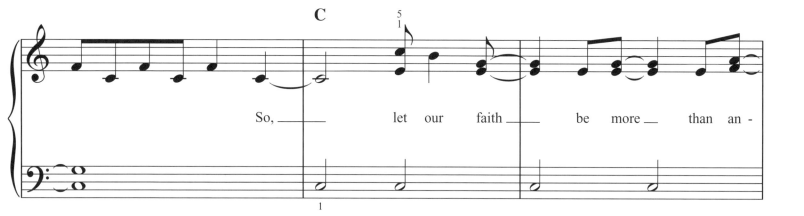

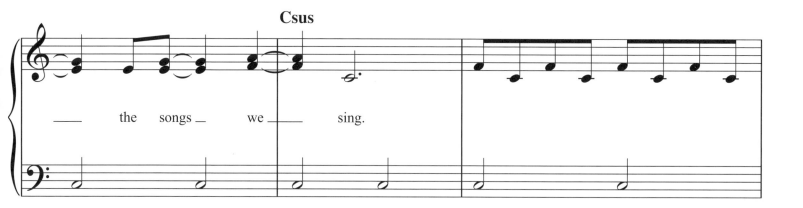

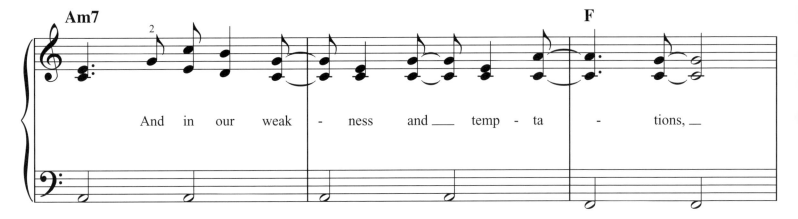

And in our weak - ness and temp - ta - tions,

we be - lieve, _____ we be - lieve. _

_____ We be - lieve ____ in God the Fa - ther, ____ we be - lieve ____ in Je - sus Christ, _____ we be - lieve _

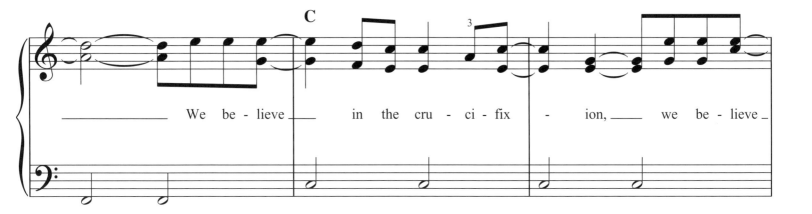

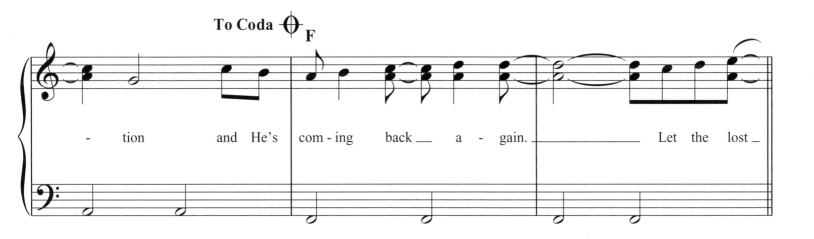

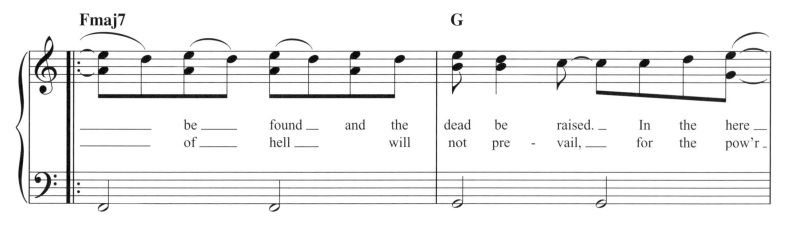

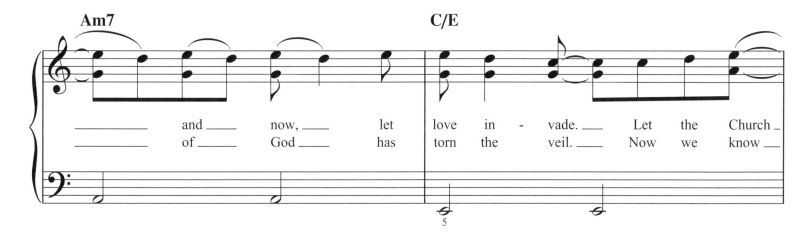

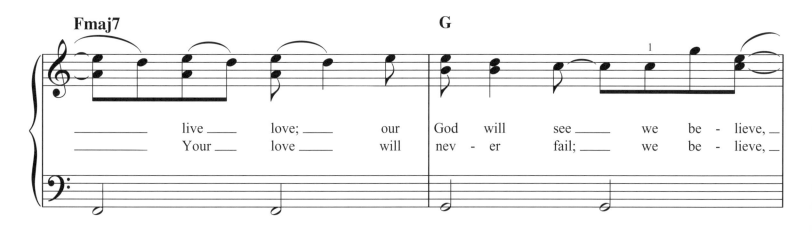

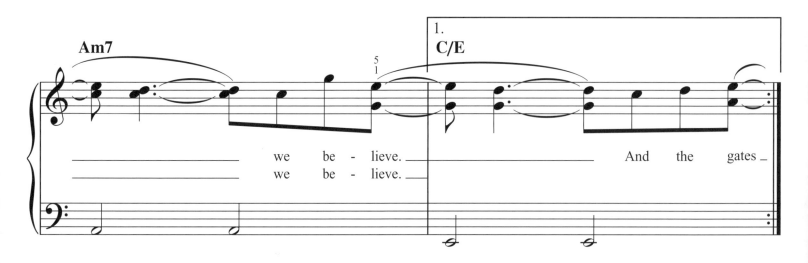

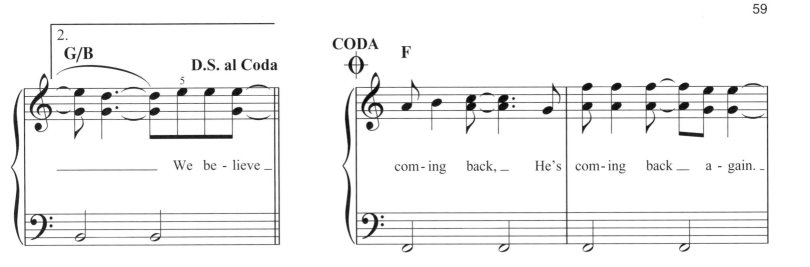

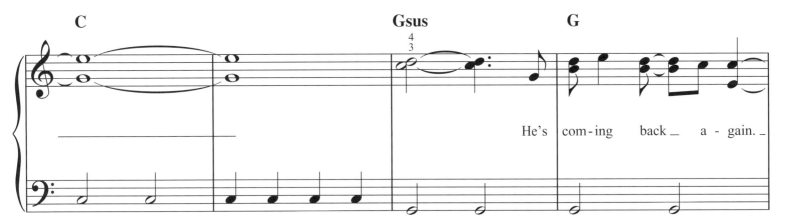

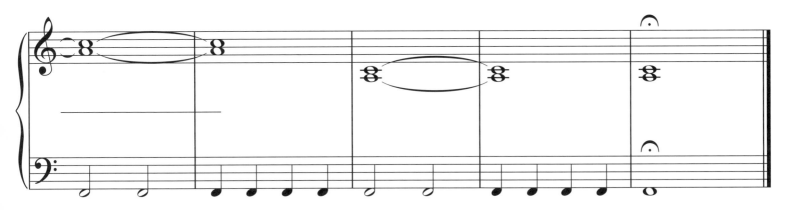

YOU ARE MY ALL IN ALL

By DENNIS JERNIGAN

Moderately slow

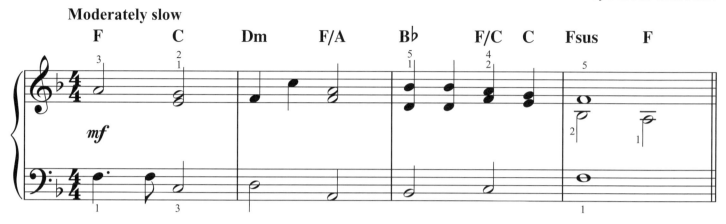

You are my strength when I am weak, You are the Treas-ure that I
Tak - ing my sin, my cross, my shame, ris - ing a - gain, I bless Your

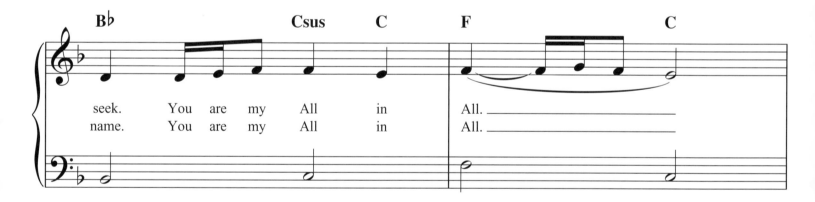

seek. You are my All in All.
name. You are my All in All.

Seek - ing You as a pre - cious jewel, Lord, to give up I'd be a
When I fall down You pick me up, when I am dry You fill my

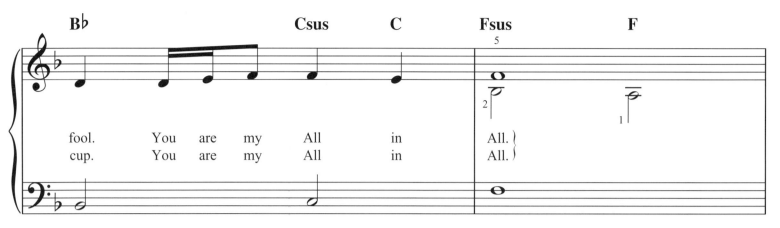

fool.   You are my All in All.

cup.   You are my All in All.

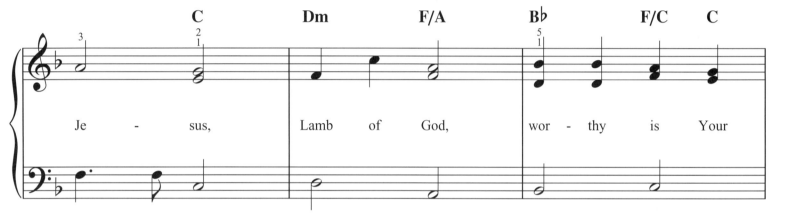

Je - sus,   Lamb of God,   wor - thy is Your

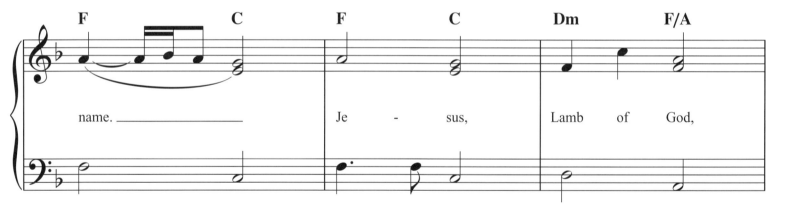

name. _____   Je - sus,   Lamb of God,

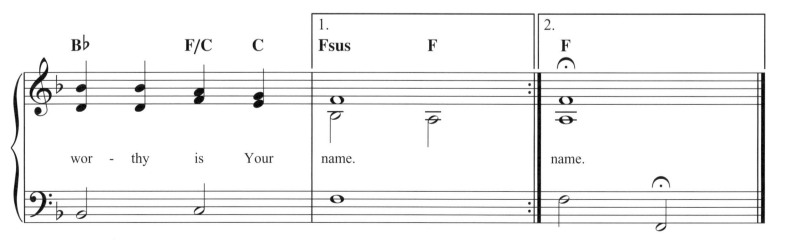

wor - thy is Your   name.   name.

YOU ARE MY KING
(Amazing Love)

Words and Music by
BILLY JAMES FOOTE

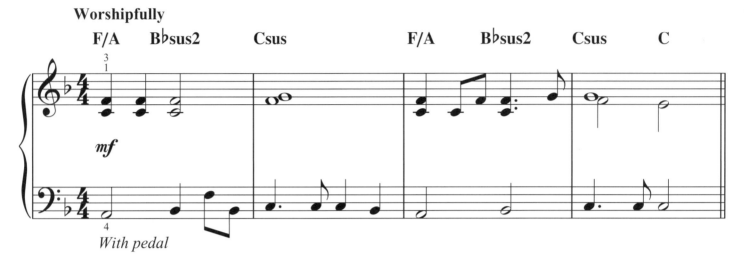

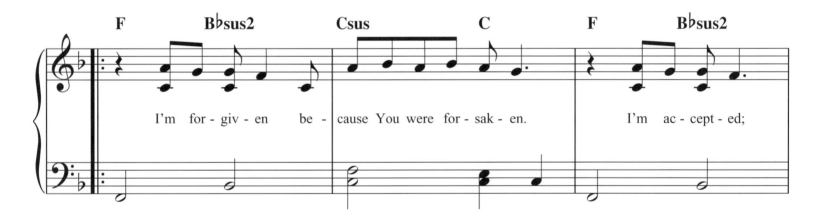

I'm for-giv-en be-cause You were for-sak-en. I'm ac-cept-ed;

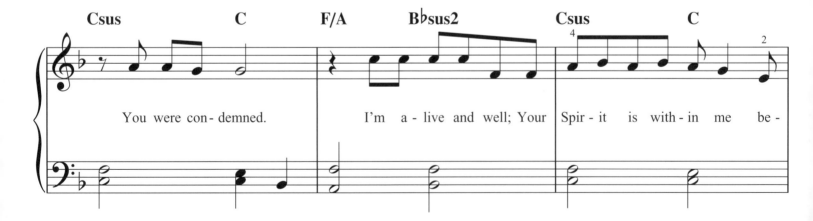

You were con-demned. I'm a-live and well; Your Spir-it is with-in me be-

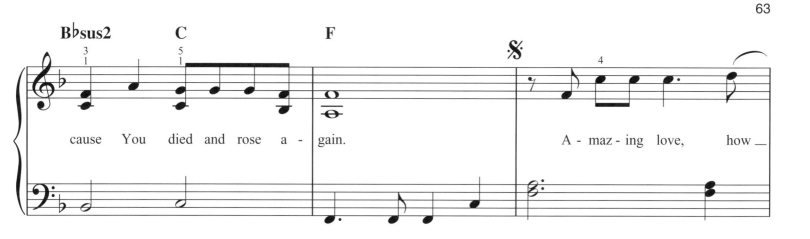

cause You died and rose a - gain.   A - maz - ing love, how __

__ can it be __   that You, my King, would die for   me?

A - maz - ing love, I ___ know it's true; __   it's my joy to hon - or

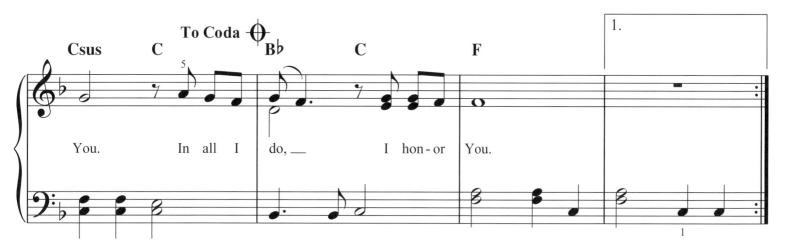

You.   In all I   do, __   I hon - or   You.

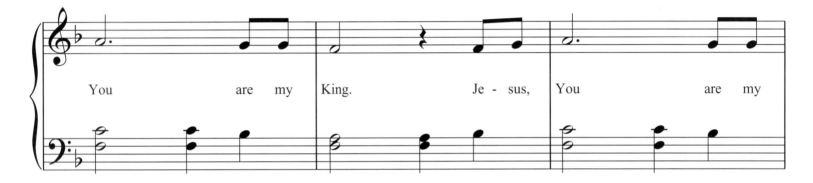

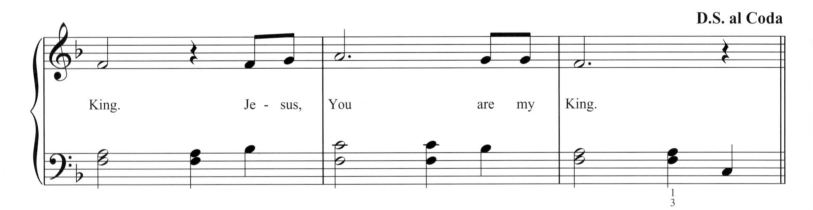

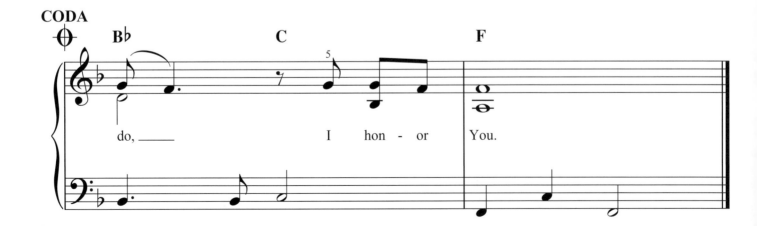